HEART TO HEART
WITH YOUR HORSE

THE HORSE-LOVER'S GUIDE TO SELF-COACHING

Caitlin Collins

HEART TO HEART WITH YOUR HORSE

Published in the UK by
Robin and Joaney How
Timberscombe
Somerset TA24 7TD

ISBN 978-0-9927105-0-7

Cover photo of Rowan and Caitlin by Sam Moore
Book design by The Write Factor

CONTENTS

Focus. • Firmness. • Don't shoot the messenger. • Key questions. • Expanding your horse's comfort zone. • Confidence boosting tips.

INTRODUCTION

Whatever amount of riding or horsemanship experience you have, the purpose of this book is to encourage and inspire you to gain greater satisfaction and enjoyment by becoming a more effective coach for yourself and your horse.

In my day-to-day work with horses and riders, I find the unifying theme underlying all the different things I do is that of helping humans and horses to enjoy each other's company. This applies whether teaching riding, starting and bringing on young horses, or tackling specific problems. It's also crucial in confidence coaching. I meet many people who are on the point of giving up riding due to having lost their confidence, and are experiencing tremendous regret and even guilt because they no longer feel able to ride or to enjoy being with the horses they love so much. Helping them to find ways forward that work for them is tremendously rewarding.

There are many ways to enjoy the company of horses without riding them. While most of the clients I work with want to ride, there are many people who have horses they don't ride, and I've written this book with these people also in mind.

Not just another riding and training manual, *Heart to Heart with Your*

Horse is less about telling you what to do and more about helping you to explore what you want to do and how you might do it. You will become more confident and self-reliant and better able to enjoy your horse's company – and, from his side, he'll enjoy being with you more!

Topics tackled include identifying your needs and those of your horse; setting goals; improving your emotional connection and communication; problem-solving; bringing out the best in both of you; preparing for success; coaching for confidence, performance and personal development; working with a riding instructor; and keeping a horse at livery. There is an appendix on new trends in horsemanship including going bitless and barefoot. And a section on further reading at the end is followed by an invitation to visit the website, with further options for meeting up with like-minded people, reading articles, taking part in courses and workshops and receiving personal telephone mentoring.

Throughout the book I have used female pronouns for the humans and male ones for the horses; this isn't to indicate any particular gender significance – it's simply to make it easy to distinguish who we're talking about. (And of course it doesn't apply when talking about specific individuals who happen to be either mares or men!) Also, I've changed names where necessary to respect people's privacy.

What exactly is coaching?

While it doesn't necessarily exclude instructing, coaching isn't quite the same thing. A good coach takes part in a shared process of exploring what works well for the client, rather than just issuing instructions from a position of expertise. The coach encourages the client to take an active part in the learning process, helping her to clarify aims, explore new things, reflect on what works well or could be improved, and come up with creative ideas for what to do differently. You could say that a coaching session is more 'client-centred' (to borrow a term from the world of counselling), meaning that it's directed by the client's

2

requirements, as contrasted with a lesson in which an instructor who has a particular area of expertise teaches a specific skill. There's a place for both approaches, of course: there will be times when you identify a particular skill you want to learn and you'll want an instructor to teach it to you.

You'll still need the instructor to be a good coach, though, so you'll find it easier to learn what he or she is trying to teach you.

Coaching yourself is similarly all about facilitating learning and making it fun, interesting, and rewarding. And since you're both coach and client, you treat yourself with the same care and consideration as you'd treat someone else.

Equestrian coaching is especially interesting because there are three participants in the relationship: the coach, the client and the horse. In addition, the principles of coaching apply in how the rider and horse relate to each other, and if you can set up the kind of learning space in which the horse feels able to participate fully then the most amazing things can happen. You can treat your horse as your client, and coach your horse. You can even allow your horse to be the coach, with you being the client; this occurs when you connect with your horse completely honestly, with the genuine willingness to learn from him and respond to what he is communicating.

Learning how to learn

The key to learning anything lies in knowing how to learn. Think of a riding lesson in which you felt tense; perhaps you were scared of the horse (a bit jumpy on a windy day), or anxious about the task you were set (those jumps look colossal), or maybe resentful of the instructor's attitude towards you (does she really think you're screwing up deliberately?) or towards your horse (hitting him isn't helping). How easy was it for you to learn? How easy was it for your horse to learn? How much did either of you enjoy yourselves? Hmm... Now remember a lesson in which you felt relaxed and inspired; or, if you

3

can't remember one (what, *never?!*), imagine what such a lesson might be like. Notice how much more receptive to learning you are when you're relaxed; when you don't have to protect yourself you can focus on learning and have the confidence to try new things.

This is the mark of good coaching: it makes learning easy and enjoyable for all concerned.

Going deeper

I believe that we're only just beginning to wake up to the multi-level possibilities of horse-human interaction, that go way beyond the obvious physical aspects of our borrowing the superior speed, strength and agility of the horse.

Most conventional riding instruction in the past has tended to focus on observable physical technique with relatively little attention paid to inner attitudes, feelings, beliefs and values. But, as today's riders are increasingly recognising the need to address the deeper, inner levels, so the equestrian world is beginning to draw on developments in sports coaching, human psychology, equine psychology, and inter-species communication. Good coaching addresses the inner levels of mind and spirit as well as the outer physical skills. And horse-facilitated coaching for human personal development is expanding the possibilities for horse-human interaction in new and fascinating ways.

NLP in coaching

Neuro-Linguistic Programming (NLP) is a practical approach to coaching that provides effective methods to work with both the inner psychological and outer physical levels. NLP can help us to improve our awareness of how we perceive ourselves and our world (the Neuro aspect of NLP), how we communicate with ourselves and others (the Linguistic aspect), and how we do what we do (the

4

Programming aspect). You could say that NLP is really about 'de-programming', as improving our awareness of habitual ways of thinking and acting enables us to explore different options, freeing us to become more spontaneous and more authentic. Enjoyment is an important part of NLP; among the criteria for assessing an NLP session, along with 'How effective is it?', is 'How enjoyable is it?'

Horses love NLP! They love it when humans are happy, and they love it when humans are moving towards greater awareness and authenticity – maybe because the humans become so much nicer to be around! Much traditional horse training has been based on correction, and punitive methods are still widely applied, including harsh use of bits, nosebands, spurs, whips, auxiliary reins, and various other gadgets of control and restraint. Imagine what it would be like to have someone tell you to do something, but make it difficult or impossible for you to carry out the order. So they punish you for not doing it. Or they issue instructions in a language you don't understand and then, as you hesitate, not knowing what to do, they punish you. As you get more confused and scared, they punish you more, until eventually, by accident, you do what they want, so they stop punishing you – and that absence of punishment is your 'reward'. Terrifying, isn't it? It's also terrifyingly common in the equestrian world.

NLP brings in a radically different perspective: drawing out the best in someone, whether human or horse, within a kind, warm approach that encourages learning while promoting confidence and enjoyment. The emphasis is on effective communication, which means enabling horses and humans to understand each other and build mutual trust, respect, and delight in each other's company.

PRACTICE

Here's a little NLP exercise for you to try. It's a reflection on the following question: *How might things be different for you, if you were to act 'as if' you believed each of the following four NLP ideas or 'presuppositions'?*

Notice the careful wording of the question. There's no need for you to believe any of the four ideas, or engage in philosophical speculation about whether or not they're true. You only need to imagine yourself acting 'as if' you were open to them as possibilities, and consider some of the possible implications of doing so.

❖ If what you're doing isn't working, do something different.

❖ There's no such thing as failure, only feedback.

❖ A positive intention underlies even apparently destructive behaviour.

❖ We are all doing our best at any given moment, even when screwing up spectacularly. (Of course we could do better if we had more resources, but meanwhile we're doing as well as we can with the resources available to us at the time.)

Take a few moments for reflection, asking yourself the question about each of the four ideas with reference to yourself and your horse, and, if you like, to your life in general.

As you go through this book you'll find a variety of ways, many drawn from NLP, for exploring options for you to change and develop as a rider and horse-person. You'll also find a chapter on horse-facilitated coaching for personal development, which encourages you to apply elsewhere in your life the insights and skills you gain with the help of your horse.

We're going to begin in Chapter One by taking a look at what's important to you with regard to your riding and horsemanship: what you want, where you'd like to go, and what you're willing (or not) to do on the way.

CHAPTER ONE:

WHAT DO YOU WANT?

What is it about horses and humans? People put vast amounts of money, time and effort into keeping horses they may ride only a few times a week. When I ask my clients what's so important to them about their horses, while a few enthuse about the excitement of riding for sport, as in competing or hunting, the majority answer that what they really value is the relationship, the connection they share with the animals.

In this chapter we're going to take a look at why you want to ride, or to be around horses. What do you enjoy most, and what's important to you about it? Considering these questions will help you to identify what's already working well for you and what changes you might like to make. This is the first step in any coaching process; it points you in the direction that's right for you – and it can save a lot of wrong turnings.

What makes your heart sing?

First

Go through the following list of possible activities and give each a number from 0 – 10, with 0 being zero interest, and 10 being Wow! You're not scoring them as current areas of expertise, but as possible activities that you might like to try if the opportunity were to arise. The suggestions are necessarily brief, so feel free to add your own details; for example, regarding cross country jumping, you may find the idea of serious eventing unappealing and give it a zero, but quite fancy the idea of tootling round a local fun ride with optional jumps and give that an 8.

I'D ENJOY…   SCORE:

Hacking out in the countryside on a lovely day,
just me and my horse   —/10

Hacking out with friends   —/10

Riding on the roads   —/10

Galloping over the hills with the wind in my face   —/10

Grooming a horse   —/10

Feeding a horse   —/10

Gaining the trust of a frightened pony, that moment
when he first dares to touch my hand with his muzzle   —/10

Schooling on the flat   —/10

Schooling over jumps   —/10

9

Having a lesson with an instructor I get on with —/10

Having a lesson with an instructor I don't get on with
but who might have something to teach me —/10

Co-coaching with a friend —/10

Competing in order to win —/10

Competing in order to take part in an event
with other people —/10

Cross-country jumping —/10

Hanging out with my horse in stable or field —/10

Watching horses playing —/10

Groundwork – perfecting half pass in hand or
on long reins —/10

Liberty playing —/10

Horse agility on the ground —/10

Riding bareback —/10

Riding with no tack at all —/10

What else? What other magic moments are there for you? Come up with as many as you can think of now, and keep adding to the list as more moments come to mind later on.

Now, if you like, see if you can expand your list of high-rated activities. Take a look at something you rated somewhere around the mid-range and ask yourself: *What would need to be in place for me to enjoy this activity even more?* For example, suppose you rated schooling on the flat as a 5. What would need to be in place for you to enjoy it more? Well, perhaps a safe, enclosed area would be nice – even just taping off a corner of a field. Perhaps you'd like to have someone there to help; could you invite a friend to come over? Or, if you need to be clearer about what to do and how to conduct a schooling session so both you and your horse enjoy yourselves, what about having some lessons or consulting some books?

Imagine yourself doing whatever it is, and, as you come up with answers to the question, 'What would need to be in place?', notice how your feelings change.

You've hit on a key coaching point: identifying what needs to be different for you to be OK in any specific situation. Of course you're not always going to be able to make all the changes you want in every case, but it's surprising how a bit of creative thinking can help in many instances.

Second

Now pick one of your high-rated activities and ask yourself the following questions. Although the activities are potential activities, not necessarily current ones, the questions are phrased in the present tense. This is because it works best if you imagine yourself actually doing the activity now, in the present moment, as vividly as you can.

❖ What's important to me about this activity?

❖ What does it bring me? Or, What does it do for me?

❖ How do I feel as I imagine enjoying this activity now?

Then go deeper with these questions, moving to deeper levels of experience and opening up to deeper levels of feeling.

❖ What's even more important about it?

❖ What does it bring me that's even more important?

❖ How am I feeling as I imagine enjoying this activity now?

Repeat this process for your other high-rated activities.

Third

Lastly, let's look at what you'd be willing – or not – to do in order to enjoy your high-rated activities. Regarding each of your top activities in turn, consider the following points, assigning marks from 0 – 10, with 0 being No thanks and 10 being Of course. Not all the questions will apply to all activities; for example 'Hanging out with my horse' involves no training – but it may require you to deal with other people's criticism if you're in a highly competitive livery yard.

I'D BE WILLING TO...   SCORE:

Make a serious commitment to training
several times a week   —/10

Travel for lessons   —/10

Travel for competitions   —/10

Get cold and wet   —/10

Deal with other people's criticism   —/10

Improve my health and fitness so I can ride better   —/10

Allow an instructor to be horrible to me   —/10

Allow a trainer to be horrible to my horse   —/10

Stretch myself beyond my comfort zone   —/10

Stretch my horse beyond his comfort zone   —/10

Use forceful training methods to make
my horse do what I want   —/10

Punish my horse   —/10

Spend money   —/10

Earn money in order to have it to spend on my riding   —/10

Again, you can adapt and expand this list to suit your own
circumstances.

Take a moment to read over your notes and reflect on what you've
learned about yourself.

Later, in Chapter Three, we're going to apply these learnings to the art
of setting goals. But before that, having asked you what you want, let's
find out what your horse might say in answer to the same question.

CHAPTER TWO:

WHAT DOES YOUR HORSE WANT?

Well, for a start, I think it's a pretty safe bet that your horse wants you to understand him – and that means you need some insight into what it's like to be a horse.

Riding involves two beings, a horse and a human. If the rider is going to set realistic goals and make wise decisions, and then communicate these effectively to her horse, she must be able to understand communication from her horse and be able to appreciate and empathise with his needs.

So, just for a moment, try imagining that you're a horse. What might it be like – both subjectively, as in how you feel as a horse, and objectively, as in how your world appears to you?

Let's start with some physical attributes.

Your eyes are on each side of your head, so you can see almost all around you. Your hearing is more acute as a horse than as a human, and your ears are moveable, so you can pinpoint the direction of sounds. Your body is immensely strong, fast, and agile. Your skin is sensitive to the lightest touch, and you can twitch your skin in response to the footsteps of a fly. You have a long tail that you can swish both to flick flies away and to express your feelings. You need to eat a lot; your gut is designed to have low-nutrient, fibrous food passing through it almost continuously and you like to move around grazing for most of the day and night. Your leg joints can lock, allowing you to doze standing up, ready for instant action if danger threatens; you only lie down to sleep for short periods during which a companion remains on watch to keep you safe.

Now for some mental and emotional ones.

You're a social being, forging strong bonds of friendship. You can communicate with your companions through sight, hearing, and touch, and also mind to mind. Your group is organised as a fluid, flexible network in which each member knows his or her relationship to the others. Good leadership is essential for the safety of the group; leadership is a changeable and subtle relationship between individuals that has little to do with physical power. As an animal preyed upon by other animals, your life depends on your alertness, lightning reflexes, speed and agility, and also on your ability to read the intentions of beings of other species: you need to know whether a predator is simply out for a stroll, or hunting for dinner with horsemeat on the menu – or even actually hunting while pretending to be out for a stroll! Like other mammals, your immediate instinctive reactions to danger include flight, fight and freeze. Flight being your favoured option, you prefer open spaces and if startled you head for open ground; you're wary of woods or closed-in areas that could conceal a predator and in which you could be trapped. Your survival also depends on your ability to learn from one experience and to generalise that one-off learning to other occasions: if you've once had a narrow escape from a lion leaping out from behind a rock, you'll always avoid anything that might provide cover for a hunter.

> Take a few moments now to really get into
> imagining what it might be like to be a horse,
> inhabiting a horse's world, with the heightened

awareness of a prey animal on the alert for potential dangers. You can soften your gaze and expand your awareness into peripheral vision so you can see further around you; and, while you probably can't swivel your ears, you can become aware of sounds and identify the direction they're coming from. Notice how being attentive in these ways brings your awareness into the present moment, and stops the background chatter of your mind.

Then, after you've returned to being a human, take a moment to notice any differences in how you experience your human world, following your brief imaginary excursion into being a horse.

Now let's consider some implications regarding the differences between the worlds of horses and humans that might be relevant to how we relate to our horses.

In terms of managing our horses, how well or otherwise do we provide for the following needs?

More or less continuous eating. Confining a horse without food causes him anxiety and possibly even physical pain; your horse's stomach, adapted to trickle feeding, produces acid constantly and he must eat to alleviate the acid build up – hence the agitation and even aggression of many horses at feeding time, and their chewing wood or biting at rugs between meals.

Companionship, friendship, and emotional bonding. Moving a horse from yard to yard, keeping him with uncongenial companions or keeping him alone – all can cause emotional and physical stress from loneliness and also lack of rest, as he can't sleep deeply without someone to look out for him.

Movement. Your horse needs to be able to move around; wild horses wander up to 20 miles a day, mostly walking and grazing, with periods of playing and resting. Restricting him to a stable or tiny paddock can send him crazy with bottled up energy. Also, your horse is a flight animal. Take away his opportunity to run by shutting him in or tying him up, and his next option for responding to a threat is to fight – and someone could get kicked. Freedom to move should also allow him to find shelter from sun, wind, rain, and flies; a field shelter is great as long as it has two doors so a junior horse can use it without fear of being trapped inside by a senior one.

Horses adapt extraordinarily well to human requirements. No wild horse would enter a cave (predators live in caves), but most domestic horses will allow themselves to be shut in a stable, and will even get into a tiny little box on wheels that whizzes off down the road so they get out in a totally different place! Amazing!

Let's turn next to some of the implications of our horses' needs and aptitudes with regard to riding.

Communication. Horses are extremely sensitive communicators. They can understand predators very well. They can also understand humans very well. In fact it's almost impossible to deceive a horse. Conflicting messages, such as when a rider pretends she feels fine when actually she's scared, worry a horse. It's better to be honest with your horse and tell him how you feel, then tell him what you need him to do: admit you're feeling nervous, and ask him to be calm and steady.

A friend of mine who has a magnificent Exmoor stallion found herself getting anxious about taking him to shows during the breeding season, when all the pretty mares were going to his head and giving him ideas. So she came up with a plan. At the next show she spent some time just chatting with him before taking him out of the horsebox. She told him how she was feeling, and explained that not only was she nervous, she was actually afraid of him because he was so powerful, and she was worried that she might not be able to manage him. Then she asked him to behave like a gentleman, and to look after her. That day, while they were in the show ring with the other stallions, one horse broke loose and careered around, sending the others crazy and causing chaos. My friend's pony remained completely calm, and carefully placed himself between her and the loose horse so she was protected. She said he was indeed a perfect gentleman, looking after her throughout the incident, and she didn't have a moment's worry despite a potentially dangerous situation.

It really does seem to be true that a horse can read your mind, and your intention, even from a distance. I remember one pony I was particularly close to as a teenager. We bought him at auction as an unhandled yearling colt, and when he was old enough I started riding him. His field was visible from my bedroom window, and as I was changing into my riding clothes I could see him grazing with the other horses, and I'd send him a mental message. By the time I'd walked out to the stable, Tam would already be standing at the gate waiting for me; I seldom had to call to him.

Clarity of intention is an important key to riding. Some people say that horses move away from physical pressure, but surely, if that were true, your horse would lie down when you sat on his back! Rather confusingly, other people say that horses push into physical pressure. I think it's more accurate to say that, whether they tend to move away from or into pressure, horses are very good at responding to intention. You can push your horse quite hard without any clear intention, and he won't move; but touch him with a fingertip, or even just look at him, with intention, and he'll move instantly. There's seldom any need to get very physical. A rider's kicking and pulling must feel horribly rude and harsh to the horse; he probably feels as you would if someone shoved and shouted at you. Good riding requires a meeting of minds, so that horse and rider become as though one being, like a centaur, and the rider's aids are just that – aids: supports that help – and are invisible to the onlooker.

Leadership and friendship. Horse hierarchy is fluid, and it's normal for the status quo to change from time to time and in different contexts. There are of course many styles of leadership. Some humans, and some horses too, adopt a bullying style of 'being the boss', in which they're quick to resort to physical violence to enforce their wishes. There are other ways of leading, some of which we'll be exploring later on, for example leading by setting an example, inspiring love and confidence, offering freedom from fear, encouraging creativity, creating a space that empowers others to give of their best, and so on. Horses value friendship, and friends are not always bossing each other about. Horses also recognise the need to look after others, and, as we saw with my friend's Exmoor stallion, they will look after humans, which raises interesting questions about 'leadership'.

Flight responses. Isn't it amazing that most horses not only tolerate people riding them, they actually take care to keep the rider on board? A prey animal wanting a predator to stay on its back; whatever is going on? Clearly we must move beyond simplistic ideas of 'prey' and 'predator'; we must move into 'friends'. My mare Brigit, who prefers to be ridden bareback, takes great care of her rider, stepping underneath to catch a wobbly one. Horses who carry disabled riders move gently and carefully even when the rider is behaving in unusual ways that might be expected to frighten a horse. Horses can set aside their flight responses to an extraordinary degree; however riders can unwittingly trigger flight in their horses by tightening up, gripping with their legs and clutching at the reins, actions perhaps similar to a predator's clinging with the claws before going for the kill. Many riders are afraid of riding their horses in open spaces, forgetting that, while we humans usually feel safer where there is cover, our horses usually feel safer in the open. If your horse gets fizzy in the open, check that you're not tightening up;

the problem for the horse might be due to your instinctive anxiety about open space. Also, a safety tip: you're much safer leading a jumpy horse with you between him and the fence. He is unlikely to shy towards the fence; he'll jump away from it, heading for open space – and if you're in his way you can get flattened.

Looking at things from the point of view of the horse can help us to be more patient and compassionate when we run into difficulties; it can also help us to find solutions that work well for all concerned. It's essential for effective goal-setting: a human who sets goals without taking her horse into account is setting them both up for problems. Effective goal-setting is the topic of the next chapter.

CHAPTER THREE:

SKILFUL GOAL-SETTING

'Goal-setting' is a term that thrills the hearts of some while prompting others to retreat like startled snails. The snails are right to be cautious – it can be a dangerous business: that's why there's a saying, 'Be careful about what you ask for – you might get it.'

For one thing, the very concept of setting goals can be overly action-oriented. As sages, artists and horses will affirm, both wisdom and creativity arise from stillness and spaciousness; it's very useful to know how to do nothing. The busy go-getter who rushes about without thinking things through can be a proper nuisance to everyone else.

I sometimes wonder how horses feel about humanity's attachment to goals. Being overly goal-oriented can lead riders to become bossy, demanding, exploitative and callous, all in pursuit of something that is meaningless to a horse, such as winning an inedible rosette.

However, for most humans, progress of some kind is an important component of living a fulfilling life, and skilful goal-setting aids progress. It gives us the clarity of knowing what we want and where we're going regarding both our larger purpose and the immediate task of the moment. It also includes considering what in NLP is happily termed 'ecology', meaning the possible consequences for ourselves and others both now and in the long term, thus reducing the risk of nasty surprises round the corner.

In this chapter we'll be looking at the principles of effective goal-setting, raising questions around what success means to you, and practising an NLP exercise that enables you to work constructively with your inner critic – that little inner voice that says, 'Yes, but…'

What would you do…?

Take a moment to reflect on this question regarding yourself and your riding: *'What would I do, if I really believed I could…?'* How you answer will tell you a lot about the scope of your vision. Some riders will go straight for the Olympics; others for being able to enjoy a gentle hack on a nice morning; while some will go temporarily blank at the radical possibility of being free to imagine what they want. (Not you – you've already prepared for this with the insights you gained in Chapter One!)

This simple question can raise some interesting issues about beliefs. Henry Ford is credited with the saying, 'Whether you think you can or whether you think you can't – you're right', indicating the importance of our beliefs in empowering or undermining our efforts. We'll be looking at beliefs in detail later on; for now, just use the question to expand your imagination enough to come up with some answers. The subsequent exercises in this chapter will help you develop your answers into workable goals.

Purpose, direction and milestones

Identifying your aims in terms of a larger purpose, a general direction and some specific milestones can be of great help in skilful goal-setting.

If you identify your purpose as your greater intention, which includes the reason why you're doing something, then your direction naturally falls into alignment with that while your milestones mark the stages of your journey.

For example, your purpose may be to improve your riding so that you and your horse feel safe and happy in each other's company and you can both enjoy hacking and taking part in some local riding club activities; this will bring you pleasure, a sense of achievement and a measure of fulfilment.

Allowing your purpose to draw you towards it will establish your direction. Is what you're doing taking you towards your purpose or not? Just grooming your horse, and in the process enjoying yourselves and improving your relationship, can become a step on the path. Any activity that you don't both enjoy, or that damages your relationship, is immediately flagged up as a possible wrong turning.

Your milestones along the way can also be relatively big or small: if jumping in your first show would be a mega milestone, an enjoyable schooling session would be a smaller one. It's important to spot many markers along the road, both so you have somewhere close enough to envisage reaching by the end of the week, and also so you can look back and appreciate the distance you've travelled.

Pure is good

Coaches often advise their clients to have pure goals. Pure in this context isn't about morals – it's an acronym! Try this next exercise: choose one of your goals, and refine it in accordance with the four PURE principles.

Positive

Have you noticed how difficult it is to follow an

instruction to not do something? Don't think of a pony up a tree. Mmm… What colour was your pony? Expressing a goal as a negative doesn't work well. If a rider says, 'I don't want the horse to run off,' the thought will arise in her mind of a bolting horse; she'll tense up, and the message she sends the horse comes across as an instruction to bolt. So what to do if you don't want your horse to run off? Ask yourself what you want instead. 'I want the horse to go quietly,' becomes your goal. Now all your actions of mind and body are in alignment with that wish. You think of your horse going along nicely, your breathing slows down, you relax – and, like magic, your horse is going quietly.

Under your control

It's fine to want to ride in the Olympics, but being selected for the Olympics isn't entirely under your control; it's up to the selectors and depends on many variables, such as you and the horse both being sound and on form at the selection events. What is under your control is your doing your best to prepare yourself and your horse to reach the required standard; and, unless you're already riding at a very high level, there's likely to be a lot of ground to cover on the way.

Right size

This point is about finding the right size of goal to motivate you, neither too trivial to bother with nor too daunting to tackle. If the Olympics would be an ambitious undertaking, a gentle hack might be relatively small. But if a hack is too much to contemplate at present, just bringing him in and brushing him could be achievable. Or, in the other direction, if the thought of schooling on the flat doesn't thrill you, ask yourself what's important about doing it – perhaps it could enable you and your horse to perform better, which would bring you more show jumping success. Now it matters enough to get you started.

Ecological

Everything we do affects others. Your riding affects you, your horse, and your friends and family (and anyone else who wants you to stay in one piece). Omitting to consider context and consequences is often a factor in the common syndrome of self-sabotage: a wise part of us is aware of a possible problem and sabotages our plans in an attempt to prevent an unwanted consequence. If this happens with you, instead of scolding yourself for 'failure', ask your inner wisdom what changes need to be made, or what safeguards need to be in place, for you to go ahead. Be willing to change your plans, and check for whole-heartedness before proceeding.

Six-step goal-setting

Experimenting with different ways of setting goals can be very helpful. I particularly like the following six-step formula, put together by a big name in the NLP world, Robert Dilts.

1   Negation: what you don't want
    'I don't want to be the sort of rider who kicks and pulls and is always falling off.' This sort of negation can be a good 'stick' motivator – something to move away from. But don't stop there, as not only does it not offer any solutions, it could even take you in the direction you want to avoid, because people tend to gravitate towards what they focus on (remember your 'not' visualising a pony up a tree in the previous exercise).

2   Polarity: the opposite of what you don't want
    'I want to become a super rider, quiet and elegant and with a seat like superglue.' Having identified what you don't want, now you ask yourself, 'What do I want instead?' Remember the importance of phrasing your outcome in positive terms, so you direct your attention towards what you do want. But, again, don't stop here: wishes aren't horses, and they don't go anywhere until you give them legs.

3   Model: an example
    'I want to become a super rider like Carl Hester.' Think of someone who has achieved the goal you want. This gives you a positive role model and, crucially, the evidence that it's possible. You can investigate how your model did it, and adopt and adapt those of their methods and their personal qualities that might be appropriate in your own circumstances.

4   Abstract: identifying some details about your goal
     'I want to become a super rider, and explore how
     far I can go with classical riding… all the Ps in place
     – piaffe, passage, pirouette, half-pass – in perfect
     harmony with my horse.' Wow, that's impressive.
     Now you're starting to build a picture of what it
     might be like to have attained your goal, and
     you're putting in some powerful positive 'carrot'
     motivators too.

5   Extending resources: increasing the qualities you'll
     need to attain your goal
     'I want to become a super rider by improving my
     health and fitness; cultivating more enthusiasm,
     perseverance and confidence; and putting more
     effort into training and practising.' You're really
     hotting up now, and are recognising that you
     already have many of the resources you need for
     the job – you just need to build on them

6   Result: acting 'as if' you had already achieved
     your goal
     'I'm riding with consistent quality in my training
     sessions: balanced, focused and in true connection
     with my horse. I'm feeling confident, buoyant,
     enthusiastic and fulfilled, knowing I'm living my
     dream.' Notice how this one brings about a real
     shift in how you feel *now*. It changes your energy
     so you find yourself naturally magnetised towards
     your goal.

While you wouldn't necessarily want to trudge through all these six
steps too often, they can be useful sometimes. Most people will tend
to favour some rather than others; try experimenting with the ones

that don't come so easily to you. And if at any point in the process you find yourself thinking, 'But I can't do that…', apply the simplest unsticking device in the world: just add the little word 'yet' – and notice what happens.

Enjoying success

Considering goals requires us to consider the possibility of achieving them – 'success'; or not achieving them – 'failure'. We're going to take a radically fresh look at the concept of failure in Chapter Six, so let's set that aside for now and make a start with success.

What do you think of when you think of success? Take a moment to consider what success means for you – first generally, then in the context of your riding.

There are different ways of judging success, aren't there? Success criteria may be quantifiable, as in how much money you earn; achievement-oriented, as in observable accomplishments; and externally referenced, as in material success that others can see and admire – the house, the spouse and the lifestyle, or the yard, the horses and the prizes.

But there are other success criteria that are more concerned with quality than quantity, as well as being more internally referenced and not necessarily observable by others. What about your own subjective experience of happiness, enjoyment, or fulfilment? Isn't that important to you?

With this in mind, try the following exercise. It starts off just as you did in Chapter One, then takes you even deeper.

> Regarding yourself and your horsemanship, ask yourself: *'What do I want?'* Let an answer come up; don't worry about whether it's the ultimate answer to end all answers, just work with whatever surfaces first.

Ask yourself, about your answer: *'And what will achieving that bring me?'*

Again, accept whatever answer pops up quickly.

Ask again, about the new answer: *'And what will that bring me?'* Whatever comes up is fine.

Go on asking the question, about each new answer: *'What will that bring me?'* Each answer you get is the right one for you at this moment and is what you work with.

Keep asking and answering until an answer arises non-verbally, as an experience or emotion that feels right for you. You'll find yourself feeling some kind of happiness or fulfilment, right now in the present moment. And that's what you're really after; the others were steps to take you to this experience.

Let's look at an example of how this exercise might go.
What do I want?
To get on the riding club show jumping team.
And what will achieving that bring me?
It'll show my friends at the yard that my horse and I aren't so useless after all.
And what will that bring me?
It will do wonders for my confidence and self-esteem.
And what will that bring me?
I'll feel great!
And what will that bring me?
I'll feel happy and energised and motivated. It feels good!

Let's stop there! The point is, if that's what you want, wouldn't it make sense to be creating that experience right now? This doesn't mean sacrificing measurable achievement. Most of us are encouraged to be task-oriented – it starts before school, with tying our shoelaces, and goes on through reading and writing to passing exams, and out into the big wide world of work and competition. But if you take care of *how you are*, then *what you do* becomes easier; or, as NLP people put it, if you can take care of your state, the task can take care of itself. And if what you want is to feel great and to be happy and energised and motivated, then it makes sense to start enjoying whatever you can do with your horse right now, and not gritting your teeth comparing your current reality with your anticipation of some far off day in the future when it might all come together!

This leads us to another, related factor that affects our experience of success. We are often encouraged to keep looking to the future and striving for the next thing. The problem is that if we repeatedly move the goal posts so they're always in front of us, we don't appreciate where we are now. We're like a pony trotting faster and faster after a carrot dangling on a string in front of his nose. But watch what the wise pony does. The wise pony stops, the string swings back and the carrot pops right into his mouth. It's sweet and crunchy and absolutely delicious. And enjoying the carrot doesn't prevent the pony from moving on; on the contrary, it nourishes him so he can keep up his strength. (Let's not push this metaphor too far, or the pony might eat so many carrots he gets too fat to move!) The point is that not only is it important to celebrate reaching each milestone, it's also important to appreciate the here and now of every moment.

Managing your inner critic

Many people find both their goal-setting and their enjoyment of success are inhibited by the presence of an over-active inner critic. We'll be looking at this problem in more detail later, when we look at the psychology of inner obstacles, however we're going to end this chapter with a final goal-setting process that can help to deal with that little voice of doubt. This creative exercise could well be called 'How to Manage your Inner Critic'; instead, it's known to NLP enthusiasts as the Disney Planning Strategy.

It is said that Walt Disney was a whiz at planning. He understood very well the common human tendency to shoot down a dream before it has a chance to flap its fuzzy little winglets. Walt came up with a constructive way to manage criticism, whether our own little inner voice of doom or somebody else's wet blanket. I've no idea if this is literally true, but the story is that Walt used three rooms for planning. His staff would dream up a wild idea in the first room, move to the second room to develop a realistic action plan, and go to the third room to present the plan to critics who would look for any flaws; then they would go to and fro between the second and third rooms until the plan had satisfied the critics.

NLP innovator Robert Dilts (he of the six-step goal-setting formula) has developed an elegant coaching process based on Walt's model, and what follows is a simplified version of his exercise. While it's possible to do it from the comfort of your armchair, it works best if you get up and follow the instructions to move around; this frees up your imagination and is more energising and entertaining. It's even better if you can get a friend to help by coaching you through the process, encouraging you and writing notes for you.

1   Label three pieces of paper as follows: Dreamer, Realist, and Critic. Set them out in a circle on the floor. Add a fourth place, Observer, to one side.

2   Taking an idea that inspires you, step into the Dreamer position and look up and far away... relax and soften your gaze... What might it be like if you were to follow your dream? What's important about it? What could it lead to? What

is enticing you forwards? How would it look?
Feel? Sound? Taste and smell? Really let your
imagination fly. Stay there long enough to feel
really motivated, then…

3   … as you move towards the Realist position turn
around twice. Then step into Realist mode. Look
straight ahead, determined, organised, enthusiastic
and energised. Now design an action plan to
bring your dream about. What steps will you
need to take to realise your dream? Come up
with a brief outline plan. When you're ready with
your plan …

4   … Move towards the Critic position, turning round
twice as you go. Then step into Critic mode.
Look slightly down, maybe with your head slightly
tilted to one side, perhaps with slightly narrowed
eyes (you know the look). Now analyse and
question the plan. (Be very clear here: you are
assessing the plan, not the dream. *Never* criticise
the dream.) How achievable is the plan, as
presented? What might be some of the likely
obstacles? Might there be any unwanted
consequences? What would need to be different
about the plan for you, as Critic, to be OK with it?
What advice would you give the Realist planner?

5   Move back and forth between Realist and Critic,
changing your physical posture as you change
place, until you have negotiated a workable plan.

6   If at any point you need a fresh perspective on the
process, step outside the system to the Observer

position and comment on what's going on. Advise
yourself on how you could make better use of this
planning process.

Whew! That's a major piece of work! By now you'll have a much
clearer sense of what you want, the direction you want to go in, and
what steps you'll need to take. In the following chapters we're going to
look at some of the ways in which you can enhance the journey for
both you and your horse, with lots of carrots for both of you along the
way.

CHAPTER FOUR:
WHAT'S IN YOUR HEART?

You could say that riding and horsemanship are mostly about relationship and communication. What's in your heart, meaning your emotional state, motivation and attitudes, is of great importance in your relationship with your horse.

Safety first

You know that safety, companionship, and good leadership feature high on the list of priorities for your horse. The better you're able to offer him these things, the more your relationship will flourish and the happier you'll both be. You need to be someone your horse is happy to be with. This isn't only a matter of being kind to your horse, it's also a matter of safety and convenience for you. A confident, happy, relaxed horse is safer for you to be around and is more willing to comply with your requests. A frightened, unhappy, or angry horse is dangerous: remember the flight or fight responses – both are extremely dangerous for any humans in the vicinity. (We'll look at the freeze response in a moment.)

Effectiveness

We've already touched on the coaching concept that if we can take care of our inner state the task can take care of itself. While this is a bit of an exaggeration, there's a lot of truth in it. How difficult would it be to ride a beautiful dressage test if you were feeling tense, angry and distracted? How much easier would it be if you were feeling calm, confident and focused? And how fantastic would it be if you were to take the next step into a state of 'flow' or being 'in the zone' – that ecstatic experience of being fully present, alert and aware, in which things just happen effortlessly, as though by themselves? How would it be if our inner state were such that options two and three could be available to us whenever we want them?

Trustworthiness

Your horse wants you to be a friend, and sometimes a leader, whom he can trust and respect. You know it's impossible to deceive him; you must be genuinely trustworthy and respectable! This means you need to be able to find the space within yourself that is authentically wise, warm and steadfast whatever is going on. (And if you find yourself wailing, 'But I can't do that', try adding the little magic word that opens the door to possibility... 'yet' – and then read on to find out how!)

Emotional intelligence

Many people are understandably wary of their own and others' emotions, having found them to be unpredictable and sometimes frightening. However, it really is possible to learn how to be at ease with our emotions and to welcome them as messengers bringing us valuable information. Riders wishing to form good relationships with their horses can't afford to overlook the importance of cultivating their own emotional intelligence, maturity and stability. This becomes especially necessary when working with horses who have been scared in the past by people's aggression, anger, impatience and exploitative attitudes; such horses require very careful and steadfast handling to regain their confidence in humans.

'Feel'

Developing that elusive quality of 'feel', so desired by riders, depends on your awareness of what's going on in your own body and mind, and also in your horse's body and mind. Emotions are called feelings because we feel them as physical sensations in the body – hence the expression 'gut-feeling'; spare a thought here for your horse, whose gut is a lot longer than yours. (This is why some people eat when they're anxious, while others can't eat a thing. Horses are similar: some practise 'worried eating' to calm the sensations in their tummies, while others won't touch food when they're upset.) Thoughts, emotions and physical factors such as muscle tension and body posture are closely connected, and the mind and the body influence each other. 'Feel' can't be reduced to just a physical technique; it requires your present-moment total awareness of the body, mind, heart, and soul of yourself and your horse. (If this sounds rather daunting, just remember that powerful little word... 'yet'.)

Unconditional positive regard

In order to work effectively with your horse, you need to be able to create an atmosphere in which learning can take place, for both of you.

Riders are often rude to their horses, calling them stupid, obstinate, lazy or difficult. They are also often rude to themselves, calling themselves stupid, cowardly or hopeless ('I always screw up' becomes a self-fulfilling prophecy). This kind of aggression is not conducive to learning. Carl Rogers, the founder of person-centred therapy (which forms the basis of modern counselling) said that a therapist should demonstrate 'unconditional positive regard' for a client, to encourage the client to feel safe enough to be open to exploring new things. Your attitude of genuine friendliness and goodwill towards your horse and yourself will create the best opportunity for you both to feel safe enough to be open to learning.

This might be a good place to mention the importance of affection: both horses and humans are affectionate creatures and need to be able to give and receive affection. Many enjoy mutual grooming – try scratching your horse's neck or withers while holding your arm out for him to nibble. And most horses appreciate a hug and a kiss; while of course kissing a velvety nose offers us one of life's great pleasures. It's curious how squeamish many people are about expressing affection to their horses, exhibiting an almost Puritanical disapproval of such displays of emotion. I don't know if it's a particularly British inhibition – I seem to remember from my days in the US that Americans were just as buttoned down in this regard. But thankfully the times they are a-changing: not so very long ago people not only didn't hug their children, but smacked them routinely before breakfast in readiness for any misbehaviour during the day!

Mirror, mirror in the stall...

Horses, with their super-sensitive ability to pick up the intentions and emotional states of other beings, will often mirror and manifest the intentions and emotions of the humans around them. It's this mirroring ability of horses that enables them to be so helpful to people who consult them in horse-facilitated therapy. It's part of what's going on when a good rider is communicating as though by magical thought-transference with her horse. It's also part of what's going on when a not-so-good rider is communicating with her horse with rather less magical pulling and kicking and shouting and tears. If your horse is behaving in ways that seem to be expressing anger, confusion, anxiety or reluctance, check what's going on inside you. It's unfair to punish him for expressing what you're feeling – and it will damage your relationship to do so. How can a horse trust or respect you if you blame him for your own stuff? Your horse requires you to be as aware of and honest about your own intentions and emotions as he himself is.

Fear and alarm

No apologies for saying more about safety here – it's important. If we want to stay safe around horses we need to know the difference between our ordinary habitual anxiety and the sense of alarm that signals real danger. For many people anxiety is a more or less constant background state; if this is the case for you, don't add to your worries by worrying about being worried – anxiety is actually quite normal for humans. But there is a difference between ordinary anxiety and circumstantial alarm, and if you're going to spot that difference you need to be attentive to your emotions, without repressing, ignoring or misinterpreting their messages. Dissing any emotion, such as ridiculing fear, is rather like shooting a messenger – it's both unkind and likely to lead to trouble. Your horse may be walking along looking positively angelic to an external observer – but if you on his back are aware of butterflies in your tummy, or a little inner voice whispering, 'Uh, oh – this could go off pop at any moment,' you would be very unwise to ignore such messages.

Water, water everywhere

Now that you're convinced of the need to pay attention to what's in your heart, along with your tummy, gut and everywhere else, let's look at some research that could indicate one possible way in which emotions might be transmitted between humans and horses, and indeed between all living beings.

We know that the bodies of mammals are composed of a high percentage of water: human bodies are over 60% water, while horses' bodies are around 70% water. A Japanese researcher called Masaro Emoto has suggested that water molecules are affected by intention and emotion. He has taken stunning photos that seem to illustrate the changes that take place in water crystals subjected to different thoughts and feelings, both directly from a human concentrating on the water and indirectly via music that conveys particular attitudes, thoughts and feelings. Beautiful, regular, complete crystals result from positive input such as love and harmonious music or melodic sounds. Jagged, irregular, fragmented crystals result from aggressive input such as anger and discordant music or harsh noise.

Mr Emoto believes that his work (which is considered controversial by many scientists) could be indicating one way in which emotions and intentions are transmitted between living beings. We literally feel it in our water molecules. Whether this is factually true or not, how differently would we behave if we acted as though we believed it? And how different would our world be? It wouldn't be just Prince Charles making friends with his flowers – we'd all be a lot nicer to everyone else on the planet, and indeed to the planet itself.

Leadership matters

Another interesting area to consider with regard to 'what's in your heart' is that of leadership. As we know, leadership is important to horses and features strongly in their relationships with each other and with humans.

In recent years there has been a growing interest in leadership in various contexts including business, the military and education. It has also been a hot topic among natural horsemanship enthusiasts. In all areas the old paradigm of 'command and control' has been challenged; such an authoritarian approach is now seen to disempower people and stifle creativity. New paradigms are emerging, tending towards more collaborative approaches which encourage the sharing of responsibility; the trend is shifting from 'power over' towards 'power with', with inspiration replacing coercion as the major motivator.

At the same time, attitudes towards animals are changing very fast; only a few years ago the concepts of animal rights, or of animals having emotional needs, or even of animals being conscious, sentient beings, were considered eccentric. Horses were generally seen as working animals to be exploited for human benefit: pulling carts, labouring as pit ponies in the mines, carrying soldiers into battle – and, when worn out and no longer useful to humans, being sent to the slaughterhouse. Nowadays I think probably most leisure riders think of their horses with affection and have a sense of responsibility for their well-being, including their happiness as well as their physical health. Many go further, and love their horses deeply as friends and fellow-beings.

For such people, the old paradigms of exploitation and force are no longer acceptable. Old-fashioned ideas of 'breaking' young horses have given way to 'starting' and 'bringing on', and new methods and systems of training, some genuinely based on empathy and kindness, are appearing. Many people, opening up to the idea that teaching is a two-way process, are finding the humility to learn from the horse, suspending the arrogant wish to 'correct' the horse and being willing instead to ask what he might be communicating.

Studies of wild and domestic horses are improving our knowledge of how horses interact with each other. Again, old-fashioned (and rather sexist) ideas about a boss stallion ruling a harem of compliant mares by brute force are giving way to observations of more sophisticated, fluid and contextual relationships among herd members. We know now that much of the leadership comes from the older mares. Physical dominance is less significant than more subtle personal leadership qualities, as a smaller animal may be senior to a larger, more physically powerful one.

All these developments in our understanding are very encouraging. However there remain many instances of bullying and brutality in the world of equitation, and, while some are blatantly exploitative, as in the horrors that go on in the training of some competition horses, others are perpetrated by well-meaning people who mistakenly believe they are demonstrating strong leadership. Just like humans, horses can respond to bullying with a range of emotional responses including anger, resentment, fear, anxiety, depression and withdrawal. Caught in a no-win nightmare where they can neither fight nor escape an intolerable situation, they may go into freeze mode, in which it's as though a part of the psyche shuts down or even leaves altogether.

The freeze response

I once bought a beautiful black Irish hunter, nine years old, who was being sold by a dealer on behalf of the MFH whose horse he had been. I kept him at the dealer's yard for a few weeks after I bought him. This horse had what many people would describe as very good manners: he would stand in his stable, completely immobile, while I mucked out; then he would snap to attention to comply with anything I wanted, such as moving over or lifting a foot, and then resume his guardsman-like immobility until further orders. One afternoon I left him standing while I went to the tack room; I also, inadvertently, left a bag of carrots on the floor by his front feet. When I got back, he was still standing exactly as I had left him, the carrots untouched. I felt tears coming up, and suddenly found myself sobbing as I looked at this horse, frozen as a statue, his natural impulses, curiosity, spontaneity and emotional connectivity all suppressed; it was as though my tears were his, the colossal sadness he could not express.

My beautiful black horse was locked into freeze mode. Fortunately, his was a relatively mild case: he thawed within a few weeks of coming home and being loved, and for the rest of his life he remained a happy, exuberant, loved and loving horse.

The freeze response is especially evident in flight animals, although it also occurs in predators, and humans, who have been subjected to trauma such as an attack or abuse or a major emotional shock. In extreme cases it's as though the consciousness partially leaves the physical body. Psychologists call it 'dissociation'. The shamanic traditions describe it as the soul leaving, with the body remaining as a sort of functional shell, like a robot. In the bad old days, 'breaking' a young horse sometimes meant just that – breaking the spirit through ill-treatment, in order to induce an extreme freeze response so the horse would be reduced to a kind of zombie that would be passively reactive, devoid of any initiative of its own. This state can last for a long time if the trauma or abuse is ongoing. If the trauma stops, the consciousness can re-enter; this is often accompanied by emotional upheaval, often including tremendous anger.

There are many degrees of freezing, and probably all of us have experienced it for ourselves to some extent when we've been in an intolerable position where we can't fight, we can't run away, we can't see any way of changing the situation, and the only option left is to mentally withdraw in an attempt to protect ourselves. Horses trained by harsh methods, especially with draw reins that force the head down, will sometimes dissociate temporarily – you can observe such horses moving in a strangely robotic manner, without sparkle or presence, and, if you look in their eyes, there's nobody home.

The freeze response in domestic horses is usually a product of a prior emotional disconnection – the disconnection of whoever has bullied the horse into this state. The human perceives the horse as entirely 'other' and lacks empathy and compassion for the animal as a fellow being, so there is a disconnection between them. There's also likely to be an internal disconnection within the human herself, as she is very probably out of touch with her own feelings as well as those of others. Sadly, such disconnection is sometimes normalised in the horse world; it's even apparent in language, when somebody refers to a horse as a 'thing', as in, 'I want to get something that jumps well,' thus depersonalising the animal and reducing him to a mere object.

The exercises we're going to turn to now all offer ways to increase our sensitivity and awareness, thereby improving the ability to connect with others – and with deeper levels of ourselves too.

PRACTICE

RELAXATION

We're going to start with a relaxation exercise. Relaxation is the foundation of the six classical scales of dressage training: relaxation, rhythm, contact, straightness, impulsion and collection. As the first of the scales, it is a prerequisite for all the others, and it also pervades all the others. There's more to relaxation than one might think: it includes flexibility, fluidity, softness, lightness, willingness, ease and an absence of 'brace' or resistance in body and mind. It requires, and is evidence of having achieved, deep trust and confidence. People often overlook the fact that it's just as important for the rider as for the horse: only if you can really relax and be at ease in your body and mind can your horse can be likewise. If you're unconsciously tense, bracing even slightly in your body or mind, your horse will be aware of it, and will be inhibited or blocked to some degree. Profound relaxation is perhaps the most important key to the magic door to that centaur-like connection that riders – and horses – so delight in.

> You can do this practice either lying down or sitting up, with your eyes either closed or open, according to your preference (and your circumstances). Take as long or as short a time over it as you like – you might combine it with a meditation practice lasting 20 minutes or more, or you might whiz through it in less than a minute.

Of course the best place to do it is with your horse, so he can enjoy it too. While taking sensible precautions to stay safe, so you don't get accidentally trodden on if something startles him, you can try it alongside your horse in the stable or out in the field. This also has the advantage of giving you the opportunity to notice how he responds to your changing state.

Start by taking two or three deep breaths as you begin to relax, then rest your awareness lightly on the process of breathing, the physical process of the breath coming and going. After doing this for several breaths, gently begin to imagine what it might be like if you could refine your awareness so that you could follow the breath in, all the way down, and then continue to follow it as the oxygen radiates out to all the parts of body, and even to all the cells of body. Let your awareness expand to touch every little cell receiving that life-giving energy, so you're aware of your entire body feeling alive and open and energised.

Now gently place your awareness down in your feet, becoming aware of the sensations in your feet, and imagine that the muscles in your feet are relaxing. Notice how it would feel if all the muscles in your feet were to relax.

Now imagine that feeling of relaxation flowing up into the calf muscles. However it feels – maybe a warmth, or a heaviness, or a tingling – just notice that feeling of relaxation flowing up into the calves, and relaxing the calf muscles. Let the relaxation continue up through the knees into the thighs, and let the muscles of the knees and thighs relax.

Allow that relaxation to flow up through the hips into the abdomen and stomach, relaxing the stomach muscles, then up to the chest, and over the shoulders, and down the back. If you're sitting up, it might feel like letting a cloak slip down off your shoulders.

Allow that relaxation to travel down the arms, into the forearms, and into the hands, so that even the fingers relax.

Now become aware of your neck muscles, noticing the neck muscles relaxing up into the jaw; the jaw muscles relaxing, and the facial muscles, the cheeks, the little muscles around the eyes, the forehead, and finally even the scalp muscles, all relaxing.

If you like, you can picture your relaxation as being like a light, perhaps a golden light, filling your body from the tips of your toes to the top of your head. Then expand it to form a protective sphere around you, so you're filled by it and also surrounded by it.

Now continue to rest lightly in that state of relaxed awareness, gently breathing with the entire body. Let the mind take care of itself, the thoughts, feelings, and sensations gently coming and going, as you simply let them pass by, just floating like a feather in the sky, relaxing and enjoying...

...until it's time to return to the ordinary world, to the activities of the day. Maybe you'd like to bring some of that light, and that lightness of being, along with you to help you with the activities of the rest of the day. Take a few moments to 'come back', and make sure you're completely alert before you start doing anything requiring full attention.

BODY AWARENESS

This next exercise is a great way to develop awareness of what's going on with the body. If you've ever been surprised by an instruction to adjust your riding position – 'Was I really pulling back with my left hand / turning my right toe out / looking down / leaning forward?' – you'll know how the body seems to have a mind of its own, often with very different ideas from yours. The exercise will also help you to notice how much the mind and body affect each other, particularly the link between thoughts, emotions and physical tension. For the horse's sake as well as our own, we need to increase our awareness of what we're actually doing rather than what we think we're doing when we're on his back.

While you can of course do this practice on your own, it's even better if you can find a friend to work with you so you can coach each other through it. The coach can prompt the practitioner with the instructions, while reminding her to stay focused and maintain the detailed commentary. The following instructions are written so they will work both if you have somebody else coaching you and if you're doing the exercise on your own.

1   The practitioner finds somewhere she can lie down
    or sit comfortably.

2   For ten minutes, the practitioner will describe
    aloud to the coach what she is experiencing with
    her body, going into as much detail as possible.
    This is to be a simple descriptive commentary of
    what is actually happening, with no judging or
    chatting about it, just describing what's going on as
    it is being experienced, moment by moment. (It
    may be easier to do this with the eyes shut.)

    Our language for sensations is quite limited, so the
    coach may need to encourage the practitioner to
    be creative, maybe describing sensations in terms
    of weight, solidity, fluidity, temperature, texture,
    movement etc, and experimenting with other
    words not normally associated with sensations,
    such as colour or shape or sound.

3   The coach will prompt the practitioner with the
    following points:

    Keep your attention on bodily, physical sensations.

    Keep talking. What's going on now?

    Move your attention around your body and
    compare different parts. For example, is one foot
    warmer than the other? Be attentive to your
    breathing... your blood... your bones... your
    internal organs... your skin... your hair... your
    nails... your cells.

Move the right leg half an inch sideways and relax the thigh muscles; describe how that feels different. And the left leg... the right arm... left arm... shoulders... neck... each time describing how it feels different. Try tightening different areas – how does that feel?

Notice, without judging, any connections between thoughts, feelings and bodily sensations.

Now let yourself think of a slight annoyance, something that irritates or mildly upsets you. Describe what's happening in your body now.

Now think of something that makes you feel happy, that delights you. Describe what's happening in your body now.

4   When ten minutes have passed, the coach will let the practitioner know that the time's up, and will invite her to bring her attention smoothly and gently back into the room. It's nice to allow a few minutes for the practitioner to tell the coach what she learned during the exercise and also to give feedback to the coach as to what she liked about the coaching, and what the coach might try differently another time.

CIRCLE OF EXCELLENCE

This next exercise is based on a classic NLP technique for finding any inner state you want, when you want it. The original exercise can be quite elaborate: this is a slimmed-down version, adapted especially for you to use with yourself and your horse. I use it frequently with myself and with clients, both human and equine.

> You can do this exercise in the presence of your horse, either standing beside him or already in the saddle. If your horse is not actually present, then you can imagine him being there so you can include him in the practice.

1   Identify the qualities you want to have in order to be able to do whatever it is you want to do with your horse eg confidence, relaxation, alertness, calmness, happiness, enthusiasm, focus etc.

2   Imagine yourself experiencing those qualities now. You may be able to draw on a memory of an occasion of having experienced them, or you may be able to imagine what it would be like if you could experience them now. However you do it, do it now, and take a few moments to really get into the experience, so that you're not just thinking about it but are actually feeling it.

3   Now imagine a circle around you and your horse, a circle that somehow contains or expresses those qualities you're experiencing. How large would you like the circle to be? (Generally, a smaller circle is more intense; it can of course move with you, like a spotlight. However it can sometimes be useful to extend it to include a larger area such as an arena.) What colour or colours would you like your circle to be? (Lighter colours usually work better than darker ones.)

4   Give your creativity free rein to enhance and
    intensify your circle of excellence. For example,
    try imagining that the bodies of both you and the
    horse are made of light of that same colour.

5   Now imagine the path ahead of you illuminated
    with that colour, so you can move forward
    together as though you were one being, like a
    centaur, moving along the path that is appearing
    before you.

You can use this exercise whenever you need to give yourself or your
horse a bit of a boost. It's great for increasing confidence under any
circumstances and also for enhancing your performance in
competitions. You can of course adapt it to suit yourself, and with
practice you'll find you can do it very quickly – you can even use it
instantaneously to bring calmness and clarity in a crisis.

In this chapter we've been focusing on you and what's going on inside
you that affects those around you, especially your horse. In the next
chapter we're going to look at how you can communicate more
effectively with your horse – which includes understanding what he is
trying to communicate to you. We'll also look further into the
principles of coaching, including co-coaching with friends, and giving and
receiving feedback, and we'll experiment with some handy questions
and techniques that can help to unstick you if you get stuck.

CHAPTER FIVE:

CONNECTING AND

COMMUNICATING

In this chapter we'll be looking at effective ways of communicating with our horses – and with ourselves.

NLP, which consists almost entirely of practical techniques, contains very little theory. However there is a list of basic principles, called 'presuppositions' (some of which we looked at in the Introduction to this book), which provide a kind of conceptual foundation for the techniques. One of the presuppositions is apt for this chapter. It states: 'The meaning of your communication is apparent in the response you get.' Hmm... I'm not sure how well it demonstrates its own principle! It's trying to say that it's your responsibility to communicate with someone else in such a way that the other person can understand, and how well you've achieved that can be judged by that person's response. So if you invite somebody to take a seat, and they walk off with your favourite chair, whose fault is that?

How does this apply to us riders?

Firstly, rather than blaming our horses for being stupid or disobedient, let's take the responsibility to be comprehensible to our horses.

This is quite a revolutionary idea in the equestrian world, where many people continue to honour the old British-abroad tradition of simply shouting louder, apparently in the belief that if you shout LOUDLY ENOUGH IN ENGLISH the stupid foreigner will eventually get it! Sadly, such riders and trainers apply increasing force, with harsher bits, tighter nosebands, bigger whips, longer spurs and more creatively coercive gadgets, in the blimpish belief that the stupid horse will eventually get it.

Secondly, let's consider the possibility that, whatever the horse is doing in response to a request, he may in fact be doing exactly what we've asked. It may not be what we wanted, but it's what we actually communicated to him.

We know that horses have a strong need for friendship and emotional connection, with a natural inclination towards the co-operative attitude necessary for happy relationships. The equine capacity for friendship extends beyond their own species: luckily for us, they're keen to be friends with humans too. Not only are horses willing to share their physical strength, speed and agility with us, they're also willing to share their minds, hearts and spirits, offering us the deep connection that can make riding an ecstatic and even spiritual experience for both horse and rider. (I believe this to be a deeper meaning of the mythological centaur. The Greek centaur, Chiron, represented healing or, literally, 'making whole', which would make sense in terms of this experience.)

So, if your horse is naturally inclined to co-operate with you, and he isn't doing what you want, it could be because you're communicating something quite different from what you think you're communicating (and remember, your horse is extremely sensitive, even telepathic). Punishing him for this is unfair, unkind and ineffective – because the problem is not his fault! Rather than trying to sort out the horse, it makes more sense for you to improve your own communication skills, leadership qualities, emotional congruence and riding abilities.

How do we communicate?

We humans are very proud of our linguistic abilities, even referring to other beings dismissively as 'dumb animals' as though an absence of verbal speech must signify inferiority. I disagree with those people who think you shouldn't talk to your horse on the grounds that horses don't understand human speech. Horses are very good at understanding non-horse beings, and can make use of whatever information is available; they can discern the emotions conveyed in the human voice and they can learn their human-given names and the meaning of specific words. Also, when we talk we express what is in our minds in words, which makes our thoughts clearer to ourselves. The horse has already picked up on what we're thinking – but we may not be so aware. Speaking our thoughts aloud allows us to notice whether we're thinking in a negative or positive way: are we saying to the horse, 'Don't bolt', or 'Please go steadily'; 'Don't be frightened', or 'It's ok, you can do it'! I find it helpful to chat to a horse, telling him how I'm feeling, explaining what I'd like him to do and asking for his co-operation in putting on his bridle, getting on his back, or whatever.

There's much more to communication than just speech. There's physical touch, body language, positioning, facial expression, laughter, energy movement and mind transmission. As we've already mentioned, one of the most important aspects of communication is the mental power of intention, to which horses seem to be very receptive.

How do horses communicate?

Communication is of course two-way, and we need to learn how to understand our horses. As social beings they are great communicators. While there is plenty of information available about equine body language, there doesn't seem to be so much said about their facial expressions. But horses have very expressive faces, don't they? In addition to the obvious movement of the ears, the set of the lips, and the wrinkle and flare of the nostrils, there are those huge and beautiful eyes. A happy horse has a relaxed face, with bright, yet soft, eyes. This expression can intensify into what can most aptly be described as a smile, as the whole face kind of lights up and lifts. The smile can intensify further into the expression of what might be called rapture, which you can see on the face of a horse who is delighted, such as when experiencing a centaur-like connection with a human: the horse's eyes glow and the face goes very smooth; the ears may be forward, or one or both ears may be slightly back if the attention is directed towards a rider.

People who are accustomed to horses may become very sensitive to how a horse is feeling. I start a lot of youngsters, and often get up on them bareback, but this doesn't mean I'm a brave rider; I'm actually quite cautious, even timid, and the older I get the more risk-averse I become. I've learned over the years to be attentive to the physical sensations in my belly: any butterflies or tightening in my tummy and I don't get on, even if the horse seems completely quiet. I wonder if this physical sensitivity is due to some kind of physical resonance; perhaps it's an illustration of Masaro Emoto's water resonance theory? Horses are herbivores, with very long guts: any anxiety, unease or annoyance they feel will manifest as tension in their guts, and maybe my gut is responding in sympathy!

All but one of the exercises that follow in this chapter will require the help of your horse. But before you head out to the field, book in hand, to request his co-operation, let's have a quick round-up of some points that will apply throughout.

Good coaching

Good coaching empowers both you and your horse. That might sound a bit worrying, 'empowering' your horse – surely he should submit to your wishes? But remember our earlier discussion about leadership. While there may be occasions when you need to take charge quite forcefully, most of the time this is unnecessary and actually undesirable. It's much more delightful for both you and your horse if you co-operate as partners, enjoying each other's company; in this gentler, friendlier paradigm you can motivate your horse by inspiring him so that he genuinely wants to take part because he enjoys it, not because he's afraid of being punished if he doesn't obey orders. Good coaching also includes 'modelling' what you want: if you are irritable and impatient, or even violent and aggressive with your horse, don't be surprised if he copies you. If you want your horse to be relaxed, confident, happy and gentle, you need to demonstrate what you want.

Good coaching includes being able to give constructive feedback. Compare the following two approaches. Which one would you find more useful?

'That was rubbish. You nearly fell off! Pull yourself together and take hold of that horse or you're really going to come unstuck.'

'Well sat – you stayed on! The super-glue is working! Let's try it again a bit slower. Take a couple of deep breaths, and smile. Sit up straighter, and steady him with your seat. Talk to him nicely, or sing a little song to help you both to relax and slow down. Well done – that's much better.'

So let's make a commitment to no bullying, and no dominance / submission methods, whether applied to your horse or to yourself. If what you're doing isn't working, stop. Don't just shout louder. Patience, kindness, creativity and humour all contribute to enjoyment, which is why you're out there in the field in the first place.

PRACTICE

HANGING OUT WITH YOUR HORSE

Let's start with an exercise in which you do nothing at all! How often do you just hang out with your horse, as friends? Many people approach a horse as though he were an item of business to tick off on a 'to do' list. There's a common human neurosis that infects many riders: we have to be constantly working, 'doing' something, and making demands on the horse so he is 'doing' something too. It must seem incomprehensible to the horse, and very unpleasant. Work is a human invention, meaningless to a horse. And yet you hear people criticising a horse, saying, 'He's lazy; he doesn't want to work', as a value judgement as though it were a moral failing on the part of the horse. How mad is that? So please take some time to visit your horse; ask his permission to hang out with him, and then, without making any demands at all, even subtly, just sit with him for a while, responding to any overtures of friendliness or other communications he might offer. When it's time to leave, thank him and say goodbye politely.

Some of the most delightful experiences I've ever had with horses have come about while hanging out in this way. My chestnut Arab, Rowan, particularly enjoys these occasions. When I sit down with him in the field or in the barn, he often seizes the opportunity to have a nice nap. He positions himself carefully so he can lie down beside me, then stretches out on his side and puts his head on my lap so I can gently stroke his face and ears. He often falls deeply asleep and starts dreaming; sometimes he makes little nickering sounds similar to the ones he makes when he sees me approaching – so I'm sitting there holding a sleeping horse who is actually dreaming of me. I find this deeply touching and feel hugely privileged by this demonstration of his trust and affection. These marvellous moments could not happen if I didn't find the time for hanging out with my horses.

WHO MOVES WHO?

This is a gentle leadership game. To begin with you might need a halter and rope, ideally a longer than usual rope; a 12 foot natural horsemanship rope is ideal. Later you can try it at liberty. You can speak to your horse and use verbal commands if you like, and also try it without speaking. While I'm a great believer in treats, and often use them, I suggest you don't use treats here. This is because the purpose of this exercise is not so much about training the horse; rather it's about your finding the leadership qualities that your horse requires of you, and feeding him treats might interfere with this process.

1   Park

> Ask your horse to stand still while you stand in front, facing him, about six feet away from him. Let the rope be long enough to allow the loop between you to rest on the ground. This is your neutral 'park' position. If your horse moves, put him back exactly where he was, then resume your position, exactly where you were. Experiment with changing your posture, body language, where you direct your gaze, and how you speak to your horse, to convince him to stand still. Notice where in your body your energy is, and experiment with moving it up and down; you may find this is related with your breathing. If your energy, and your breath, is high in your body, imagine breathing out through your legs, down into the ground. Imagine your feet are rooted in the ground. Notice any tendency on your part to move in response to your horse's movements. What happens if you hold your position?

2   Back

Gently pick up the rope a little, just enough to let your horse know that you're going to do something. Ask your horse to take just one step back away from you. This is not about forcing him backwards aggressively so he backs away in alarm. See how gently you can ask. Experiment with waving your arm at him without intention... and simply lifting your energy and looking at him with the intention that he should step back. By all means ask verbally. See if you can inspire him to step back without your having to move towards him or touch him. If you do have to touch him, see how light that touch can be... just a feather touch... Be sure to relax any pressure the instant he complies. Notice your horse's emotional responses to what you're doing. Is he annoyed? Is he scared? Is he waiting for you to make some change within you that will inspire him? Is he floating effortlessly back, his eyes shining with pleasure at being invited to dance?

Return to your neutral position for a moment. If either you or your horse feels like reaching out to touch the other, that's fine. Remember you can both smile. You're supposed to be enjoying yourselves!

3   Forward and stop

Gently pick up the rope again. It should still be slack, but clear of the ground so the horse knows you're going to do some more dancing. You're going to ask him to take one or two steps towards you, then stop before he reaches you. Make sure you've given him enough room to do that. Again, experiment with how gently you can ask him to step forward, and how gently you can ask him to stop. Notice how your gaze influences him; most horses will stop or move away if you look them in the eye in any but the most gentle and loving manner; they seem to find it rude or even threatening. Try looking down, smiling in a warm and welcoming way, and drawing him towards you by slightly hollowing your tummy, or making a tiny beckoning movement with one hand in front of your tummy.

Park again; and a quick snuggle if you like. One of my clients does what she calls 'huggins buggins' with her two Dartmoor ponies; they all enjoy it!

4   Quarters over

Gently pick up the rope slightly. Now you're going to ask your horse to move his hindquarters away. First, step gently towards him, and put your hand on his neck; keeping your hand on his body, move along until you're level with his hip, then step back away from him and look at his hindquarters with the intention that he should move his backside away from you. If necessary, try moving your hand towards him, or wiggle the free end of your rope towards his bum. Again, experiment with the gentlest possible communication to inspire him to float his hindquarters away from you. As a variation on this exercise, ask him to make a turn

on the forehand by touching his side where the
rider's leg would touch him; no more than a
feather of a finger-touch, and release the pressure
the moment he moves. Do this exercise in each
direction.

Each movement requires you not only to invite your horse to move,
but also to allow him to do so: if you're restricting him with the rope he
can't move, any more than you could perform a yoga stretch with
someone hanging onto a rope round your neck. Coach yourself to
apply the following sequence as you practise these exercises, and notice
how much easier it becomes for both of you to dance.

❖ Stand firm

❖ Invite

❖ Allow

❖ Enjoy

Notice that at no time is there any thought of 'making' the horse do
something. You don't 'make' your dance partner do anything (I hope!)
– you invite and inspire him to enjoy dancing. And remember the
importance of constructive feedback: there's absolutely no room for
rudeness to either yourself or your horse. Simply notice what's
happening, run experiments, have fun, and enjoy developing your
self-awareness and your powers of observation and improving your
ability to communicate with your horse.

I like to use this game with clients' horses when we first meet; it's a
good way of establishing communication and beginning the relationship.
And while we've so far talked about practising it unmounted, you can
also ask for the same movements when on your horse's back:

essentially it's just stand still, a very gentle reinback (just one step), turn on the forehand, start and stop. The exercise is also useful when starting youngsters: when you're confident sitting on the young horse as he is standing still, before you ask him to move forward, ask him to move his quarters sideways, one step at a time, and then take just one or two steps backwards. This gives him a chance to get used to your weight and also to the touch of your legs before venturing forward. There's something very calming for the horse about bending his neck and body, softening his jaw, and stepping under with the hind leg. It's also physically easier for you to stop a horse taking off if you keep his neck bent.

You can find more ideas for similar relationship-building activities on the ground in the Parelli seven games, and also in the 'dancing with horses' that Klaus Ferdinand Hempfling demonstrates so elegantly.

CHANGING COLOURS FOR TRANSITIONS

Do you remember the Circle of Excellence exercise we did at the end of Chapter Four, where you created an imaginary circle of a particular colour to help yourself and your horse to feel relaxed or confident or whatever? Well here's another way of visualising colours to help you communicate with your horse.

This exercise came about few years ago when I was asked to fill in for an absent instructor at a Pony Club rally. I had to be creative – and very determined – to get the children to stop kicking their ponies (a task made even more difficult by the parents shouting encouragement along the lines of 'Go on darling, kick him really hard – no, hit him, *hit* him, *make* him do it!'). I came up with a game in which each child had to ride around the arena following instructions to walk, trot, stop, and turn, while communicating with her pony in such a way that the other children, all watching like hawks, couldn't spot what she was doing; any kicking or pulling would bring on gleeful howls from the hawks and lose points for the culprit. To help the riders to do it, I taught them the following visualisation practice.

You can do this exercise in an arena, or in the field, or even just out hacking. You don't have to be riding; you could be long reining, lunging, playing at liberty, or even just leading your horse on a loose rope.

Imagine a coloured line on the ground going out ahead of your horse, along the track on which you want him to walk. Imagine the line stopping ahead of you at the point at which you want your horse to stop. Practise walking and stopping a few times, accompanying the visualisation with the lightest possible aids. See if you can do it with no physical aids at all.

Now you're going to trot. Imagine your line changing colour ahead of you at the point at which you want the horse to start trotting. The more vividly you can visualise this, the easier it is for your horse to pick up the image. When you want to walk again, visualise the line changing back to walk colour ahead of you at the point at which you want to walk. As before, accompany the visualisation with the lightest possible aids or no aids at all.

Now try varying the speed and energy within each gait by brightening and softening the colours. Keep reducing your physical aids until they're just not needed any more. You might like to try some experiments linking the colour changes with your breathing, so you make your transitions on the out breath, sort of breathing your horse into walk, or trot, or halt – and notice what happens. Or link the colour changes with singing to your horse, varying your singing to match your requests. Be creative and make it into a game, like those Pony Club children did, so you both have fun with the practice. The more subtly you can communicate with your horse, the more responsive he'll become, and the more you'll both enjoy yourselves.

There was an amusing follow-up to the rally incident: a few months later I met a woman who, when she learned that I taught riding, told me a story of how her daughter had gone to a Pony Club rally where there was a new instructor who forbade the children to kick their ponies and got them all following imaginary coloured lines on the ground. She finished the story by saying, 'And, you know what, the amazing thing was that, although the instructor was completely mad, Emily really enjoyed herself and discovered that she actually didn't need to kick the pony after all!'

WHAT'S IT LIKE TO BE YOUR HORSE?

Did you ever play at being a horse when you were a child? My friends teased me at school because when they were running I was cantering! Well here's a chance to play at being a horse again – with the 'grown-up' aim of improving your horsemanship. This is a game we sometimes play in my rider coaching workshops; it provides an opportunity for exploring creative communication, practising coaching skills and gaining insight into the horse's experience. The game works well with a group of three people, so if you can round up some uninhibited friends to join you, that would be ideal. If you're on your own, it works well if you imagine yourself taking each of the three roles in turn. You don't need your horse's help for this exercise, although it's nice to do it out in the field so that he can watch – it's an easy way to amuse and entertain him!

The purpose of the game is to explore communication and find out what it's like to be your horse.

The purpose of the task is to provide a forum for learning (so accomplishing the task is not the most important thing).

In a group of three people:
one person is the horse;
one person is the human;
one person is the coach, who is coaching the human.

The coach and the human, out of hearing and sight of the 'horse', decide on a task. The task is for the human to get the 'horse' to do something; this can be anything that the 'horse' would be capable of, such as walking sideways, or trotting over a pole.

The human makes contact with the 'horse' and attempts to accomplish the task by influencing the 'horse', without speaking in English. The coach coaches the human to help her to do this. Be creative:

the human can be creative in how she communicates with the 'horse';

the 'horse' can be creative in how she responds to the human;

the coach can be creative in how she coaches the human.

Useful coaching interventions might include questions such as:

What might you try differently ?

What are you learning about communication?

How might you change your energy or emotional state? (What about trying a circle of excellence, breathing differently, smiling etc?)

Feedback is an important part of the exercise:

the coach gives feedback to the human;

the 'horse' gives feedback to the human (they're now speaking to each other);

the human gives feedback to the coach.

Constructive feedback might include:

questions that invite self-assessment, such as, What do you think went well? What are you most pleased about? What might you try differently another time?

observations of the things that you thought worked well, that or you liked;

suggestions for things to try more of, or differently, another time.

> Do three rounds of the game so everyone gets a
> turn in each role.

Students on the workshops often remark on the insights they gain into how it might feel to be a horse: first of all you have no idea what the human will want you to do when she comes to get you, then you realise that she wants something but you don't know what it is; you can't understand her, and you're scared that she is going to get angry. Many students report feeling anxious, even really frightened. It gives them a better sense of empathy with and compassion for their horses, and an appreciation of their own responsibility to communicate comprehensibly and be patient if they don't immediately get the desired response.

With all these games and exercises, you need to keep in mind your aims: they are less about achieving particular tasks, more about providing opportunities for you to improve your communication skills, and for you and your horse to get to know each other better and to enjoy yourselves. If you want to have fun riding, it makes sense to practise having fun now, not putting it off for some far-off future, as in 'I'm going to work my butt off now so that one day, when I'm jumping round Badminton, I'll be happy.' You could say that happiness is a habit, in that the more you cultivate it, the easier it becomes. This doesn't rule out the hard work necessary in order to be able to jump round Badminton in three years' time, but there's no need to put your enjoyment on hold – you can have that right now, every step of the way.

CHAPTER SIX:

WHAT'S BEEN STOPPING YOU?

If you've established your goal, time has passed, and you're no nearer achieving it, *what's been stopping you?*

Notice the phrasing. We could have asked: What's stopping you? That's a good question too. But by putting the question in the past tense, we're beginning the process of putting obstacles behind us.

However it's asked, this question puts us on the spot. While we may initially blame delays on outer circumstances, such as lack of time, money or suitable facilities, our biggest obstacles are likely to be internal. I'm no longer surprised by how many people, including apparently high-powered achievers, admit to being beset by self-doubts, rampaging inner critics and destructive voices from the past. Thus demoralised, we can perceive even minor challenges as insurmountable problems.

This is not all bad news of course: it means there's always work for coaches! It also means that most of us could benefit from learning how to coach ourselves more effectively.

Reframing

Positive reframing is a skill much encouraged by coaches. It means looking at a seemingly problematic situation from a positive and empowering point of view. For example, when you have a setback, you could view it in several different ways. You could dramatise it as a disaster and go into an emotional tailspin. You could calmly remind yourself that setbacks are a normal part of life, smile bravely and carry on. You could ask yourself the question: *What could I learn from this, if I wanted to?* Notice the careful wording of the question: the *'if I wanted to'* will ease you past any awkward part of your mind that doesn't want to co-operate.

Each of these responses is a 'frame' of your own making. It's often more helpful to reframe a setback as a learning opportunity rather than as a disaster.

Fear

We've already seen the NLP presupposition, itself an elegant reframe, 'There's no such thing as failure, only feedback'. Fear of failing is instilled in most of us at an early age, with mixed consequences. If fear of failing to negotiate a sharp corner at high speed on wet ground induces you to slow your horse down from a flat out gallop it's a blessing. But, less helpfully, fear of failing can hold you back from fulfilling your dreams.

If a healthy fear of failing is to be balanced by an equally healthy willingness to have a go, the ability to reframe our mistakes is crucial. In the Practice section of this chapter you'll find an exercise to help you see mistakes as learning opportunities – as we did as children, taking tumbles while learning to walk, and learning from them that we needed to take smaller steps, or adjust our balance, or hold on to the handrail when climbing the stairs!

In Chapter Four we looked at the significance of emotions with regard to horses and riding. Now we're going to consider specifically what is probably the most common emotional issue for riders: fear, which may manifest anywhere along a spectrum ranging from mild apprehension all the way to screaming terror.

Fear is normal, right and proper: it keeps us safe. Someone who didn't experience fear wouldn't last long. For many women, fear naturally intensifies after having a child; it's as though nature wants to heighten a mother's awareness of risk, perhaps in order to keep her safe and available to look after the child. Fear can also increase around the menopause; this may be a strategy to limit activities during a transitional period in which the woman is temporarily more vulnerable. While it's always both ineffective and unkind to beat yourself up for being fearful, it's even more so in these biologically influenced instances.

As we know, horses are extremely sensitive to human emotions. Any doubts you have, your horse will know about, and trying to deceive him just makes matters worse. A lot of so-called misbehaviour in horses actually stems from the unacknowledged fear or other emotions of their riders.

A horse may respond to the rider's fear in several different ways. He may reckon that you're in no state to be a suitable leader, so he feels unsafe and becomes frightened. He may mirror what's going on with you: if your horse appears fearful or agitated, look to yourself! He may wonder what you're scared of – and think there must be something dangerous nearby that he should also be worried about. It's also possible that he may understand that your fear is your own thing, nothing to do with him or the environment, and respond by looking after you, gently taking the initiative to keep you both safe; this happens quite often, indicating that it's a mistake to apply simplistic ideas of leadership to the potentially complex relationships between horses and humans.

We've already seen the key question to ask yourself when fear arises with regard to your riding: *What would need to be different for me to be OK with doing this?* As with any coaching intervention, you need to ask this question kindly, with genuine interest, to encourage answers to come up.

You can apply the same question to your horse if he is anxious about doing something: *What would need to be different for him to be OK with doing this?* Taking an intelligent and compassionate approach to his concern works much better than punishing him for not doing what you want.

Getting back to your own fear, it could be that whatever you're anxious about just isn't going to be OK whatever you do – you simply don't want to jump any more, or ride along a main road with fast traffic, or hack out alone on a jumpy youngster. That's fine. It can be a relief to acknowledge that you're not prepared to do it any more. It frees you up to enjoy doing what you are happy to do.

Other things are not so cut and dried and there's room for negotiation. You might like to take another look at the questionnaire in Chapter One, in which you started exploring possible changes that would enable you to enjoy more activities with your horse.

As a general principle, it's true to say that if you ride better, your horse can go better, and you can both feel more confident. Good riding starts with a secure seat and a positive attitude; both are required if you are to work with your horse and not against him. Lessons are not just for competitive riders. They are helpful for all riders, to enhance your enjoyment of the riding you love.

However, riding instructors are seldom well-placed to help you to address limiting beliefs and self-doubts stemming from your past, so you may find coaching or counselling more useful to help you with such issues.

The physical health and fitness of the rider is an area often overlooked by both riders and riding instructors. Your stiff back or achy joints will affect your riding, which will affect how well your horse can go, which will affect how confident you both feel. As we get older, trips to the chiropractor and acupuncturist increase, along with yoga classes, Pilates, Alexander Technique lessons and, eventually, oh no, fun and fitness classes for the young at heart...

It's important to remember that there is always help available; nobody has to struggle alone with problems and setbacks. However, while it's good to ask other people for help and suggestions, do remember that it is your responsibility to decide whether or not to follow their advice or accept their help. Be discerning! Some years ago, when I was living in the south of England, I asked a locally well-known natural horsemanship expert for help with my horse. She started off by smacking my sweet and friendly mare in the face 'to teach her to respect the human's space'. I am ashamed to say I let her carry on – whereupon she chucked the poor mare under the chin with the heavy metal catch of the lead rope to make her go backwards. I didn't invite the woman back – but I should have stopped the lesson immediately she began bullying my horse.

The principles of good coaching apply just as much to coaching yourself as they do to coaching somebody else. Genuine interest, coupled with kindness, will get better results than denial or aggression ever did. Let's apply them in the exercises that follow. None of these exercises requires a horse, although it can be fun to practise them in the field or stable with your horse present: he will probably let you know how much he appreciates your efforts!

PRACTICE

SEVEN PROBLEM-SOLVING QUESTIONS

Let's start with some constructive questioning. The following seven questions are slightly adapted from Tony Robbins's Problem-solving Questions. Tony Robbins is an American motivational coach who is famous for his fire-walking events. The idea is that after you've walked on fire, you can handle anything. Several years ago I went to one of his weekends, walked on fire, came home all, um, fired-up, and went out to the field and got on a horse I'd been scared of. Sure enough, she recognised the difference in me and behaved like an angel. So I can recommend fire-walking!

But for now, let's stick with these seven problem-solving questions.

❖ What could be good about this problem?

❖ What is not great about it yet?

❖ What are my aspirations for change about this problem? How do I want it to be?

❖ What are my aspirations for changing myself with regard to the problem? How do I want to be?

❖ What would I be willing to do, for the situation to be the way I'd like it to be?

❖ What would I be willing to stop doing, for it to be the way I'd like it to be?

❖ How could I enjoy the process while I make the necessary changes?

I recommend thinking about these questions repeatedly over a period of days or weeks, making notes of your insights – and reading your notes to remind yourself to take the appropriate action.

FINDING SOLUTIONS IN THE FUTURE

Sometimes we might wish we could see into the future – it would be easier to know what to do if we could foresee the likely results. While foretelling the future is tricky, the good thing is that we can use the power of our imagination to imagine possible future outcomes in order to help with present problems. Here is a creative exercise in finding solutions in the future.

> Think of a current problem or question regarding your riding or horsemanship.
>
> Now imagine yourself having jumped forward to a point in the future at which you have resolved the problem satisfactorily. Describe to yourself what's going on in this imaginary future scenario.
>
> Next, in your imagination, from your vantage point in the future, look at the actions you took that have brought you this satisfactory result. What did you do?
>
> If you like, you can explore several alternative imaginary futures and the possible decisions and actions leading to them.

PARTS DISCUSSION

The next exercise involves talking to yourself, which is always interesting. It's a great way to resolve inner conflict, as when part of you wants you to do something, but another part of you would rather you didn't. There are several more or less elaborate ways of doing the exercise; this is a brief version.

> 1   Identify the riding or horsemanship issue you want to work with. It needs to be something you can think of in terms of an inner conflict as in 'Part of me wants to do something, but part of me

doesn't', or 'On the one hand I want to do it, but on the other hand I don't'.

2   Sit down and put your hands on your knees, palms up. Which part would you like to put on which hand?

3   Describe the two parts. What would each one look like, if you could see it? What would it sound like, if you could hear it? Give each part a label or a name.

4   Now you're going to have a chat with each part. Which one would like to go first? Reassure the parts, if necessary, that this is going to be a nice experience.

5   Whichever part wants to go first, ask it this question: *'What is your positive intention for me?'* Give it time to answer. If it's taking all day and you want to finish in time for tea, you can prompt it gently. Then invite it to say a bit more, allowing time for the answers, with further questions along the lines of: *'And what would achieving that bring, that's even more important?'* or *'What's beyond that, that's even more important?'* Keep going until the part has reached a constructive intention for you that feels right to you; it's likely to be something along the lines of wanting you to be safe, or to be happy.

6   Repeat the process in point 5 with the other part.

7   Draw the attention of the two parts to the fact

that they both have positive intentions. They may even want the same thing, and just be going about it in different ways. The point is that they are not enemies or opponents; they are allies, both trying their best to look after you.

8   Now you can bring the discussion to a close by asking the two parts to acknowledge the fact that they are allies by connecting in some way. Bring your hands closer together to allow them to do this. Notice what's going on as the parts make the connection, and notice any changes to their individual appearances, or if they merge into one. Whatever they do is fine. Then bring your hands up to your chest and pop the parts back into your heart, where they belong.

9   Notice how your understanding that these two parts are allies, working together on your behalf, has changed your view of the original issue and reduced or even resolved that old inner conflict.

This is a powerful exercise. You may get interesting dreams or other indications of changes taking place at a deep level of the mind.

WHAT DO I NEED?

The next exercise works best with some physical activity, as moving about can generate insights and bring about shifts more effectively than the armchair approach. It's based on a comprehensive and sophisticated process called the SCORE model, created by Robert Dilts and Todd Epstein, which is helpful for identifying blocks and problems and indicating solutions.

(Past)   (Present)   (Future)

CAUSES   SYMPTOMS   OUTCOME   EFFECTS

REQUIRED RESOURCES

1 Write the above five labels on pieces of paper and put them on the floor in the same layout, the right distance apart to allow you to step from one label to another.

2 Decide on an issue you'd like to work with regarding your riding or horsemanship. Identify a goal you'd like to achieve in relation to this issue.

3 Stand on Symptoms, facing the future. Think about your present situation regarding the problems you're experiencing in attempting to achieve your goal. Describe what's happening – or maybe not happening, as the case may be.

4 Move forward to Outcome. Describe the goal you would like to achieve.

5 Move forward to Effects, the results of achieving the goal. Consider the consequences of achieving the goal – how it will affect you and others.

6 Move back to Causes. Ask yourself, 'What has been stopping me from achieving my goal?'

7 Step over to Required Resources. What inner and outer resources do you need in order to achieve your goal? This means your own skills and

qualities, and those of your horse; facilities such a
suitable riding environment and training; and other
resources such as money, time, help etc. Imagine
having all those resources now.

8   Taking all your required resources with you, return
     to Causes. Notice what changes for you as you
     stand at Causes with your resources; notice how
     different you feel now that you have what you
     need.

9   Taking these changes with you, return to
     Symptoms. Notice what has changed; again,
     notice how different you feel.

10   Now that you're free to achieve it, step into your
     Outcome. Experience what it's like to achieve
     your goal. How does it feel? How does it look?
     How does it sound?

11   Move to Effects. Experience what it's like to enjoy
     the benefits of achieving your goal.

12   Step off the system and make a note of what
     you've learned. What practical measures do you
     need to take to acquire or gain access to the
     resources you need? Identify your first step and
     put it in your diary now!

LEARNING FROM EXPERIENCE

Based on a process developed by Robert Dilts, the following exercise is
a good method for reframing our mistakes and learning from them. It

isn't recommended for anything that might bring up intensely painful memories as in traumas or phobias, which need a different approach.

Part One

1   Think of a past occasion when things didn't go quite the way you'd hoped. It can be a recent incident or one from long ago. Make sure you have an attitude of open enquiry and willingness to learn so you can work with it now.

2   As you bring the incident to mind, imagine seeing it in front of you as though you were watching it happening on a screen. If it's something that disturbs you now, make the screen very small, and, if necessary, make the images black and white. Replay the incident several times while you watch. Notice what you did and what happened; and notice which aspects were under your control and which were not under your control.

3   Identify what you were trying to achieve at the time.

4   Now consider how you would have liked the episode to have gone. What would have been different had it gone the way you had hoped for? With the benefit of hindsight, imagine different ways in which you could have acted that could have contributed to different outcomes. Experiment with various possibilities on the screen in front of you, to come up with some options that could bring about the result you had been trying

to achieve. Be creative: imagine consulting a wise
mentor for suggestions as to what to try, and
experiment with options that go beyond your
'normal' limitations.

5   When you find an option that works well and that
    you're happy with, run it through again several
    times on the screen, watching how the incident
    unfolds differently now.

6   Now imagine that you can step into the movie and
    run through the scene again, this time participating
    in it, so you're no longer watching it as an
    observer but you're actually living it. Replay it
    several times with you as a participant, reliving it,
    with the replays speeding up, faster and faster.

7   Whew! Come to a rest. Take in all the learnings
    you've gained as you let the screen dissolve.

Part Two

1   As you relax after absorbing the learnings and
    dissolving the screen, recall an occasion that went
    well for you, something you're happy to
    remember.

2   Imagine yourself reliving that incident again now,
    enjoying those good feelings again

3   Notice what you're doing in that event that is
    contributing to the event going so well. What are

you doing? How are you being? What word or
phrase comes up that encapsulates the experience
for you?

4   Recall some other similarly delightful occasions
from your past. Notice what they have in
common in terms of what you're doing and how
you're being.

5   Consider what you might learn from these events
that you could apply in your life now and in the
future. Imagine yourself enjoying some possible
occasion in the future in which you're acting,
thinking, feeling, being and experiencing in
accordance with these learnings.

Take a moment after completing this exercise to consider some
implications of what you've learned. You'll have noticed how quickly
the exercise encouraged you to move on from what may have started
out as an uncomfortable place – remembering something that didn't go
well – to a relaxing and enjoyable experience. NLP exercises are
usually enjoyable, partly because it's more fun that way, and partly
because it's easier to learn when we're relaxed and happy.

In this chapter we've focused on dealing with what's been holding you
back; in the next chapter we're going to look at two things that can
draw you forward: learning from others' expertise and building on your
own achievements.

CHAPTER SEVEN:

BRINGING OUT THE BEST IN YOU

Having been so busy in the previous chapters, filling in questionnaires, setting goals, solving problems and doing exercises, we're now going to take a little rest. Let's take a deep breath, relax, sit comfortably, sip a cup of tea, and consider the wisdom of the East: the Taoist concept of *wu wei*, or effortless action.

'Must try harder' was a constant theme throughout my school days, echoed even by the teachers of subjects I was good at. Conditioned as we are by our work-ethic culture to apply more effort, it's hard to resist authority's imperative that we 'must try harder'. But Taoists, horses and other wise people think differently.

Let's look at the following model of four stages of competence.

- ❖ Unconscious incompetence: this is blissful ignorance — since I don't know that I don't know, I'm not trying at all.

- ❖ Conscious incompetence: a rude awakening — now

that I've realised how little I know, I must try to improve.

❖ Conscious competence: careful now – gritting my teeth and holding my breath, I'm trying hard to get it right.

❖ Unconscious competence: easy peasy – I can get on with it while simultaneously chatting and checking my phone messages, with relatively little effort or attention required for the task.

So far so good, but what comes next? What's the next level?

❖ Excellence: this is blissful presence – I'm 'in the zone'; things are just happening, beautifully, as though by themselves; it's an experience of 'flow', a kind of effortless action in which I'm fully aware and attentive but with no strain.

Experiencing that level of Excellence gives us a taste of what the Taoists call *wu wei*. While spiritual adepts take it to profound levels of deepening familiarity with the Tao, it can be found to some extent in any instance of mastery. Far from gritting their teeth with effort, a true maestro makes a task look easy. To a large degree, excellence is a matter of getting out of the way and letting the process happen without our interference. This is a key insight in learning to ride well. It's one we need to remind ourselves of over and over again, because we humans seem to be predisposed to interfere. You can set yourself and your horse up for success by asking him to do whatever it is you want, letting him do it, and sharing the enjoyment. It really can be that simple – which is why my favourite personal reminder is: Invite, Allow, Enjoy. If I could remember to remember my reminder, I'd be more likely to experience those magic moments of excellence more often!

Modelling

Excellence is a topic of great interest in NLP. The founders of NLP, Richard Bandler and John Grinder, were intrigued by how someone could achieve excellence, rather than just competence, in any field of endeavour. They found people who excelled in various spheres, and developed the art of modelling these maestros so they could teach others how to do it too.

As young children we learn by modelling those around us in smiling, talking and walking. Later we realise that we need to know more than can be gleaned from just watching and copying observable techniques; we realise that inner knowledge and also the inner state of mind are also relevant. In fact excellence is as much about inner being as it is about outer doing. In NLP, the outer doing is referred to as the surface structure, which can be observed, and the inner being is called the deep structure, which requires investigation.

There are two useful 'as if' principles to bear in mind with modelling: firstly, if one person can do something, others can learn to do it too; and secondly, we all have vast innate potentials for excellence. Although I don't know if these statements are factually correct, I do know that learning becomes easier if we act 'as if' they are.

While modelling takes place naturally as we are influenced by other people (for good or for ill – we can model bad habits as easily as good ones), there are ways to enhance the process, and we'll be experimenting with an NLP method of modelling in the Practice section of this chapter.

Inspiration

Let's look now at another important issue: inspiration, which both you and your horse will need if you're to bring out the best in yourselves.

Without inspiration, what would we do? We'd probably survive OK from one day to the next. But there's more to life than just day-to-day survival.

How do you feel when you're inspired? There's big difference between doing something because you want to do it, and doing something because you feel obliged to do it, isn't there?

Inspiration energises you and makes you think 'I want to do that.'

You can develop the seed of inspiration regarding your riding by asking yourself what's important about it. Why does riding, or being around horses, matter so much to you? Really think about it, and allow yourself to feel energised and enthusiastic about it. *That's* why you do it!

Now imagine sharing that inspiration with your horse. In your mind's eye see him full of enthusiasm, his eyes shining, his steps springy: there's true impulsion for you!

Inspiration is the starting point of every great endeavour. Start small and think big, and who knows what you can achieve?

Well done you!

Encouragement is the close companion of inspiration. Building on positive strengths and achievements works better than focusing on shortcomings and mistakes. Being a good coach for yourself and your horse requires you to develop the skill of appreciating your positive points and encouraging both of you with praise.

Notice any little triumph, however small, and say to yourself: 'Well done you!' Make a game of it: how many 'Well done yous!' can you score in a day? Start with getting up in the morning, getting dressed, leaving the house – you get the idea. Notice how doing this can make you smile, and energise you. Extend the practice to your horse, to help him to feel good about himself as well. (It's possible to take this too far. A friend of mine who was very keen on praising her pony for the tiniest achievement loudly praised him with an enthusiastic 'Well done, Jack!', when he poo-ed in a neighbour's driveway... right next to a sign saying No Horses. The neighbour, who saw and heard all, was not amused.)

People power

People power is the power of enlisting the support of a group to help with achieving goals. Of course it isn't a new idea. It goes back long before it was popularised in the business world in 1937 by the entrepreneurs' guru Napoleon Hill. He advised his students to form 'mastermind alliances', saying that when two or more minds come together they create a 'third, invisible, intangible force' – the mastermind.

Enlisting the support of somebody else permits co-coaching, which is something you might like to try with your riding. It can be more fun to go through the exercises in this book with a friend alongside you; it can also be more fun for both you and your horse to school and hack out in company.

There are several different options for co-operative people power. For example, mentors are experts in a particular field and can advise you in that area, while coaches facilitate whatever it is you want to do, helping you to bring out the best in yourself. Action-learning sets are groups of people who meet to encourage each other in learning or studying a specific skill or subject, while project teams meet to work on a particular task. Or, less formally, you can just get together with a friend or two.

All these collaborations offer benefits, including encouragement and support, the sharing of information and expertise, help with goal setting and focus, the opportunity to contribute to others' development, and feedback.

This last point, feedback, is important. We can't escape it: life gives us feedback all the time. There's a language pattern, used in NLP, called the feedback sandwich. It's a skilful way of critiquing someone's performance while simultaneously encouraging them – unlike the wet blanket sort of criticism which extinguishes any spark of enthusiasm. Here's how it works.

Suppose you need to give someone – or even yourself – feedback on a task. You can make a three-layer 'sandwich', like this:

First, say what you liked about what they did.
Second, say what you would have liked them to
do 'even more'.
Third, say something else you liked about what
they did.

Notice the careful phrasing in the sandwich filling: 'even more'. You can apply this to anything, even to something they shouldn't have done, if you're clever about it. For example you could say, 'I wonder if, another time, you could be even more accurate?' Or, 'Perhaps it would have been even better if you'd allowed even more time to complete it.' Put like this, your feedback can draw their attention to an area that needs improvement, while still being encouraging. While it's important to give people honest feedback, it really is possible to do so kindly.

Current communication technology makes finding and forming peer groups easier than ever before. If you'd like to set up such a group for your riding, look for people with similar values, but with enough variety to keep things interesting; you want to learn something, not just agree with each other. The most important factor is the genuine commitment to mutual support, so that all the members can trust each other.

Leverage

One of the most important functions of group support is to help you to move from thinking or talking about something to actually taking action. It's a common human tendency to stick with what's familiar and resist change. Motivating someone to change is perhaps the biggest issue in coaching.

So far in this book we've emphasised the carroty end of the carrot-and-stick motivational spectrum. However, in fairness to the topic of bringing out the best in you, it has to be said that stick motivation can be useful and 'leveraging your pain' can be just what you need to get moving.

Leveraging your pain might sound like a service advertised by an S and M club, but it's not as sinister as it sounds. It's actually recommended by quite respectable coaches. It means that you identify your problem and then increase your discomfort by thinking about its further implications. Suppose you have a problem with your horse. Perhaps you're not riding him very much. Truth be told, you've had a few scares, and now you're too frightened to get on him. Let's work this up. The financial costs of keeping a horse are colossal. This horse is costing you a fortune, and you can't even ride him. You haven't been out on him for three months and you're running out of excuses. How long is this going to go on? Another three months? A year? Until one or both of you are too old for riding? How do you feel about the situation? Don't you feel a bit of a wuss? What does your timidity say about you? It's a problem in other areas of your life, too, isn't it? Ouch! You're really feeling very uncomfortable about this problem now; so uncomfortable that you have to do something about it. Now you're highly motivated to find solutions – and take action!

You get the idea. Leveraging your pain hurts a bit – but in a good way! So now let's take action with a practical exercise: an NLP method of modelling.

PRACTICE

MODELLING

Modelling isn't about trying to remake yourself as a clone of your model; it's about an effective way of learning that will enable you to fulfil your own unique potential. Here's a simple yet systematic way to do it.

Identify a clear goal, such as being able to ride a

beautiful canter transition. Then find someone who is really good at it to model. (Be careful to pick a model whose methods won't trample your values; it's no good choosing someone whose methods you wouldn't want to use.) Now you're going to find out how they do it, while being attentive to the differences that make the difference between excellence and mediocrity. You can do this very simply in just three steps.

❖ Observe your model's technique. Watch them attentively; then imagine yourself in their place, doing what they're doing.

❖ Chat with your model to find out about the 'deep structure' – their attitudes, emotional states, and motivations concerning what they're doing. What are they thinking? How are they feeling? Why are they doing it? Don't assume you know – ask them! I was surprised by the answer when I asked a no-nonsense horse-dealer what she felt was the most important attitude to have for riding: 'Love,' she said; 'you've got to love the horse, really and truly love him.'

❖ Run some experiments in which you ask them to imagine omitting specific elements of their process to find out which ones are essential and which can be left out. Ask your model, 'What would happen if you didn't do that?' This enables you to streamline and simplify the process, which makes it easier for you practise it.

❖ If you have more than one model, identify the

common factors; they're likely to be important. If
there are some conflicting points, you may need
to clarify them by questioning your models.

❖   Now practise what you've learned, remembering
the 'deep structure' as well as the physical actions.

You can also work with an absent or 'virtual' model. Identify your
absent model and either imagine watching them doing whatever it is
you want to learn, or, even better, check them out on YouTube. Then
imagine yourself in their place, looking through their eyes. How exactly
are you standing / sitting / moving? Notice what you're thinking and
how you're feeling as you're in the role; you may get some interesting
insights.

It's also possible to model your own excellence. Think of something
that you do well; it could be an aspect of riding, or it could be
something else. Imagine yourself doing it now. Notice how you're
moving, what you're thinking, how you're feeling; all the qualities you
associate with this familiar occasion. Most people trying to learn a new
skill seek technical proficiency first, after which confidence and
enjoyment may follow. Try reversing that: find the confidence and
enjoyment you experience in doing something you're already good at,
and bring those states with you into learning your new skill. A
constructive emotional state enables you to act more effectively in any
circumstances, and it's much easier to learn when you're relaxed and
enjoying yourself. Practise this repeatedly in your imagination, so it
happens easily when you actually physically engage in your new skill.
    A few years ago I noticed that I was riding my mare, Brigit, much
better than I rode my other horse, Rowan. I was scared of Rowan
– who could fire up fast with little provocation – and I had a tendency
to ride him in a 'survival seat', which kept me on his back in a storm,
but probably precipitated some of the upsets due to my being a little
tense and also slightly behind the movement. So I decided to model

the way I rode Brigit and transfer it across to riding Rowan. I noticed the following important factors with regard to Brigit.

❖ How relaxed I felt around her before riding her, and how happily I looked forward to riding her.

❖ How relaxed and happy Brigit was in expectation of our riding; how willingly she would lower her head for the bridle, her eyes soft and shining, and how she would position herself by the mounting block so I could get on easily.

❖ How when I was riding her I sat in a relaxed way and we moved together easily, as though one being, each sensitive and responsive to the other.

❖ How the experience was joyful, fully in the present moment, and with a kind of lightness of being that was wholly delightful for both of us.

❖ How I could easily give the experience of riding Brigit a colour: it was golden, warm and glowing. I imagined we were both made of golden light, held within a golden circle.

This process let me identify the differences between the relaxed and joyful way I rode Brigit and the tense survival seat I was inflicting on Rowan. It also enabled me to identify what I needed to transfer from Brigit to Rowan. The golden circle was especially helpful as it contained everything I needed to transfer across, so I could use that image when riding Rowan and everything else would sort of fall into place. Sure enough, the storms subsided as my fiery little chestnut and I began to relax and enjoy ourselves – and to trust each other more.

CHAPTER EIGHT:

PUTTING IN THE GROUNDWORK

In this and the next two chapters we'll be referring to the coaching skills that were introduced in previous chapters, and looking at how to apply them in practice with your horse, first on the ground and then while riding.

PIPAR

It can be helpful to have a structure in place for a schooling session. Many people say they find schooling boring because they don't know what to do; they trot about for a bit – and then what? So I'd like to offer an idea for structuring schooling sessions based around six coaching elements: Purpose, Intention, Preparation, Activity and Reflection: PIPAR. I know that's only five – I'm OK at counting up to 10! The sixth element is Enjoyment, which is present throughout. These six elements can be applied both to the practice session as a whole and to the individual activities that take place during the session.

Notice the word 'practice'. Let's scrap the idea of 'work', whether human or equine, in these chapters. The word 'practice' has a different feel. Musicians and dancers practise, as do doctors, therapists, tennis players, yogis and meditators. And so do riders and their equine colleagues.

Let's look at how your groundwork practice might go, within the framework of the elements, remembering that the sixth one, Enjoyment, is present throughout.

Purpose is why you're doing whatever you're doing. Let's say that you're a bit short of time, and you want to do something with your horse that won't take too long, will be enjoyable for both of you, and will enable you to help your horse to practise cantering on a circle. He particularly needs to practise adjusting his balance and freeing up his left shoulder so he can take the left lead, which he finds more difficult than the right. So your purpose for this particular groundwork session is to improve the canter, and the activities you engage in will come under the umbrella of this purpose.

You'll also have a larger purpose, of course, such as bringing out the potential in your horse to become a wonderful riding horse. As we saw when setting goals in Chapter Three, a larger purpose draws you towards it and establishes your direction so that you know where you're going with each step along the way.

Intention is what you want to do with regard to each activity – or, more accurately, with regard to each moment. If you move your hand towards your horse without intention, he knows he doesn't need to do anything; but if you raise a finger with clear intention, he'll respond. It's a combination of clarity in the sense of knowing what you want, and meaning business so that it happens. It's also a combination of lightness and seriousness. The lightness is the lightness of a feather, a breath, or an angel's wing-tip (and, as you know, angels can fly because they take themselves lightly...) The seriousness is that of taking yourself and your horse seriously as the magnificent beings you really are, with all the potential you have for manifesting that magnificence.

As we've seen in Chapter Five, when the two of you are profoundly connected, just your thought will be enough: your horse can respond so instantaneously it's as though you're one being. This is a marvellous experience for both of you; I don't play any musical instrument myself, but I imagine it must be similar for people playing in a really great band, with all the musicians so connected with each other that they are playing as one entity.

Preparation sets both you and your horse up for success. It makes it easy for your horse to do what you want. It applies large-scale, to your whole session; small-scale, to each activity; and micro-scale, to each moment of each activity.

If you want to lunge your horse, your large-scale preparation will include having the proper equipment, correctly fitted, and a suitable place to lunge him in. Battling with inappropriate equipment while sliding about in the mud in an open field on the side of a hill with loose horses careering around is unlikely to get good results!

Your small-scale preparation applies to the specific activity of asking him to move round you in a circle. It would include standing in the centre of the circle and positioning your horse correctly in relation to yourself, being clear as to your intention, handling the lunge rein and whip efficiently, and using the proper body language and verbal requests so he can understand and comply with what you want. Then it's easy. However if you're unclear about what you want, faffing about with the rein and the whip while standing in the wrong place and looking in the wrong direction, you're making things difficult or even impossible for the poor horse, however willing he is.

Your micro-scale preparation applies moment-by-moment throughout the activity, as you stay mentally and physically present and actively taking part in the interaction between you and the horse. Whatever is occurring in each moment is a preparation for the next moment, which in turn prepares for the next moment, and so on. This kind of micro-management requires close attentiveness, although it is happening so fast that it's largely unconscious. If you think back to the stages of competence mentioned in Chapter Seven, you'll remember the fourth stage, unconscious competence; this is the stage at which the micro-scale preparation is happening as though by itself. This is very good – and it can get even better as you move into the fifth stage, which is excellence.

Activity is the action you're both engaging in. It could be moving the horse in a turn on the forehand, luneging him in a circle, practising leg-yielding in hand, or relaxing his jaw in response to the bit. You also need to chunk down an activity so that each of its component parts becomes an activity in its own right, even literally one step at a time. For example, in rein back, you ask for a step, then momentarily relax your aid before asking for the next step; then you gradually improve the flow of the process until it becomes one continuous movement. That momentary relaxation of the aid tells the horse that he is doing the right thing; if you just kept the aid on when he is responding, he'd think, 'Help, I must be getting it wrong – this isn't what she wants,' and you'd be well on the way to damaging his confidence.

Reflection is your personal feedback process. You need to reflect on what's going on during the session as well as afterwards. Take frequent breaks during the session to rest and to reflect. Regarding how you assess 'success', beware of being overly focused on accomplishing tasks; remember Enjoyment – both yours and his – and ensure that you don't sacrifice that on the altar of task-oriented achievement. Reflection is an opportunity for you to ask yourself what you're pleased about, and then what you might like to improve or change. Your horse is giving you feedback continuously. If you don't like what he's saying, ask yourself what you could do differently to elicit a different response. If you do like what he's saying, ask yourself what you're doing that's eliciting this response, so you can build on it.

Remember to be encouraging and constructive towards both your horse and yourself; whatever is happening, you can learn from it. It's also useful to remember that if your horse is not doing what you want, he may in fact be doing what you're asking. If so, there's no point reprimanding him: you're the one who needs to change. Perhaps the most common fault is to ask the horse to do something while inadvertently blocking him, for example asking him to walk towards you while you're staring him in the face – which to a horse is rude, rude, rude! Hence the importance of the middle part of the handy little reminder: Invite, *Allow*, Enjoy.

Let's look now at a couple of examples of groundwork practice, so you can see how the six elements might appear in real situations. See if you can spot them in these accounts.

I have just 15 minutes available to do something with Rowan before it gets dark on a winter's evening. I haven't done much with him for several weeks, and would like to start riding him again in the coming week, so I want to use this session to re-establish our connection in readiness for riding. Also, I want Rowan's help with some lungeing exercises. I've been asking clients to invite their horses to spiral in and leg yield out on the circle and to change the rein by coming across the circle in front of them – so I want to practise these exercises myself.

We go into the arena, and I turn Rowan loose to let off steam. First thing is to roll in the sand! Then he wants to play at liberty, trotting and cantering around. He is so beautiful, this little chestnut Arab, I love to watch him – he moves as lightly as Legolas the Elf, who left no footprints in the snow in the Lord of the Rings. After a few minutes he trots up to me, eyes shining, and invites me to play with him. We do Spanish walk together (a pair of Monty Pythons Silly Walking), and some side-passes, a few twizzles and a twirl – almost a do-si-do.

Remembering what I'd set out to do, I take the lungeing rein and tie it in a loose loop around his neck; I pick up the lungeing whip, face in the direction I want him to go, and say 'Walk on.' Rowan walks and trots and then canters on the circle until I ask him to slow to a trot again and invite him to spiral in and leg yield out a few times. Then he offers me a joyful canter, one ear forward, one turned toward me, his eyes shining; when I call to him he stops instantly, then as I draw him towards me, switch the lunge line and whip over (oops – a bit clumsy there), and turn to face the way I want him to go, he swings across the circle in front of me in walk, and canters gracefully away on the other rein. We do this a couple of times, delighting in the dance, then finish by sharing some ginger biscuits – Rowan's favourite treat – and he blows gently on my face with warm gingery breath. What a pleasure – we're both smiling! Next time I need to be quicker at sorting out the change of hands with the lunge line and whip when changing the rein across the circle.

Now let's visit Chris and Martin. Chris is a client of mine. Martin is an ex-riding school cob who was subjected to severe abuse, including being blindfolded and whipped by the riding school proprietor. Chris rescued him, but on getting him home found him to be too dangerous to ride: ignoring any attempts by the rider to direct him, he would alternate between baulking and bolting, which, not surprisingly, terrified Chris. It has taken us over a year of weekly sessions to get Martin reliably rideable both in the arena and out and about on the lanes and tracks.

In the early days, our priority was to establish a mutually trusting relationship between Martin and Chris and also Martin and me. A typical session would go like this. Chris would start by grooming him all over, to help him get in touch with his body; he was so shut down he was almost numb, physically and emotionally. Then we'd all go out to a round pen, and do some moving around and stroking with a lungeing whip. This was to help to reawaken Martin's physical awareness and responsiveness; also to develop his trust in us as we demonstrated that the lungeing whip was just an arm-extension and would never hurt him.

The suggestion of lungeing absolutely terrified Martin, as did long-reining, so after a few unsuccessful attempts Chris and I realised we had to abandon convention and get creative. We came up with the idea of lungeing each other, with Martin watching. At first he was horrified; then he became intrigued; finally he very timidly asked if he could join in. So we had several hilarious sessions with one of us standing in the middle like a circus ringmaster while the other scampered round in circles, followed by the enormous Martin. Gradually Martin gained the courage to go in front, and soon he was brave enough to go round by himself. Finally we were able to attach the lunge line to his halter – and Martin was lungeing like a pro.

We also did some clicker training with Martin, and of course we always gave him lots of treats. This gave him the confidence to try volunteering things, which was a major shift for this poor bullied horse, who had shut down his natural intelligence and spirit in an attempt to protect himself from abuse. He actually seemed to grow in height as he grew in confidence. It was as though he had been trying to shrink away to avoid punishment, then gradually began to stand tall in his rightful power and pride as a magnificent big black cob. He is now progressing well with his schooling both in-hand and under saddle.

I hope it's coming across here that there's so much more we can do with our horses than just riding them. Your groundwork practice sessions can span a wide range of activities. Liberty play, clicker training (see the Further Reading section at the end of this book for where to find out about that), agility (similar to that for dogs, but for horses), lungeing, long-reining, in-hand exercises, going for walks, and just hanging out together – all can be fun and educational. Attitude is key: a round pen can be a place of ordeal or delight, depending on the human's approach. Some people play games with their horses that are no fun for the horses, being more like the way a cat plays games with a mouse. Treats are great – why ever not? I would be suspicious of any trainer who claimed that horses aren't interested in food, because if a horse is not interested in food he is probably distracted by fear – which rings warning bells about the trainer. I'm also wary about talk of 'de-sensitising' horses. Huh? You want to increase his confidence and steadiness, and you might think of that as 'de-spooking' if you like – but please don't think of de-sensitising your marvellously sensitive horse, who is quite capable of reading your mind and responding to your thoughts.

PRACTICE

PIPAR

Let's set up a simple practice session: meeting up with your horse in the field, putting his halter on, and going for a short walk with him, either in the field or out and about.

Notice how we really are starting at the beginning here, with meeting up with your horse in the field. Not 'catching' your horse. Cats catch mice. Predators catch horses. Friends and colleagues meet up or get together. It's important to be careful with words, because not only does what you say express how you're thinking, it also influences your further thoughts and your attitudes – to which, as you know, your horse is sensitive. It's difficult for your horse to be confident about meeting up with you if he's feeling like a mouse being pursued by a cat.

Purpose

So, remembering that Enjoyment pervades all the elements of your session, let's consider your Purpose. Why do you want to meet up with your horse in the field? Think about it in terms of your immediate purpose and also your larger purpose. You might consider the obvious practicality – clearly it's something you need to be able to do in order to be able to do anything else with your horse. You might also think about the other benefits, such as the two of you having an opportunity to enjoy your friendly relationship and to practise connecting and communicating.

Intention

Your larger intention is to meet up with your horse in a friendly way, put on his halter, and go for a short walk. Be honest and open about this. Creeping up on him with the halter hidden behind your back doesn't deceive him – it just makes you look shifty. Be aware of equine expectations of courtesy. Having greeted him in a friendly way with your hand held out to his nose, and given him a nice rub on the neck, it is polite for you to stand beside him and put the halter on from the side. Don't come at him head-on, holding it out in front of you; it's confrontational. And don't stare at him; it's rude.

Preparation

Your earlier preparation would have included getting a suitable halter and rope, and perhaps a carrot. Wear gloves if there is any likelihood of your horse pulling on the rope when you're leading him. If there are others in the field you may need to take a stick to keep them away from your horse, and be careful about handing out any food in case it precipitates quarrelling.

Your preparation for haltering your horse will

include standing in the proper place alongside him and having the halter ready for him to put his nose in it. It's no good your horse obligingly lowering his head for the halter, only to find it in such a muddle that he can't put his nose in the loop. Presented with such incompetence he can be forgiven for rolling his eyes and sighing before walking away in despair!

Activity

You're in the right position, the halter is ready, and you know what you want. Your horse will probably be so impressed, and so confident in your competence, he'll lower his head for you to put the headpiece around his neck and place the open nose loop invitingly under his muzzle. Hey presto, he accepts the invitation to pop his nose in the halter and all you have to do is fasten the headpiece.

Reflection

Well that was easy, wasn't it? And just look at the horse – his eye is soft, and he's smiling. In fact you're both smiling! Next time you can be even more confident about the process, and even more dextrous in your handling of the halter as you pop it on and fasten it up.

Now you can apply all these principles to going for a walk with your horse: it could be walking back to the stable yard, or round the field, or out along the lane if that's appropriate.

Experiment with how to lead your horse – how to position yourself, how to position him in relation to you, how to give him the right length of rein, and how to invite him to accompany you without either pulling on the rope or crowding into your space as the two of you practise starting, turning, stopping and varying the pace. It's like practising heel-work with your puppy at dog-training classes. Make sure you can lead him equally easily from either side, and when you build up to walking past scary things make sure you are between him and the monster, both to reassure him (the monster will stop to eat you first) and also so you're not at risk of being run over if he shies.

Find out what you need to do, and how you need to be, to achieve the connection that manifests as him floating effortlessly along beside you with the rope conveniently slack at all times.

Remember to apply the coaching skills you've learned. Constructive self-talk can be helpful, repeating reminders such as Invite, Allow, Enjoy. What about creating a circle of excellence for you both, and walking along a visualised line? Experiment with practising your modelling skills, both to help you to achieve the excellence you want, and also to demonstrate to your horse what you want him to do and how you want him to be. Pay attention to the feedback your horse is giving you, both the obvious feedback – is he doing what you asked? – and the more subtle feedback – does the expression on his face indicate that he is happy about it? And pay attention also to the feedback your own body and mind are giving you – how are you feeling, both during the activity, and afterwards, on reflection?

Practising like this with a simple exercise, such as leading your horse, will give you the chance to gain confidence as you familiarise yourself with your coaching skills. You'll be able to apply what you've learned to pretty much everything else you do with him, both in groundwork and when riding.

In the next chapter we'll practise some specific exercises as a warm up for riding, before we hop up for a ride.

CHAPTER NINE:

PREPARING TO RIDE

A groundwork session can be a complete practice in itself, or it can form part of the warm-up for riding.

It's surprising how limited many riders are in thinking about the warm up: if they bother with it at all, they think it applies only to the horse, and then only to his body. Warming up is as much about the mind as the body, and it applies to the human as well as to the horse. The older I get, the more warming up I need: those hip joints just don't flex as freely as they used to, nor do the knees – and as for my increasingly creaky mind...!

There's a saying beloved by the business world – it's worked to death in beef-up-your-business seminars – that goes like this: To fail to prepare is to prepare to fail. Sorry. It is a bit tiresome. It is also a bit true. The better you prepare yourself and your horse for any activity, the more likely it is that the activity will go well.

Preparing to ride – a cautionary tale

The steps preceding your ride are not just tiresome preliminaries to rush through as fast as possible. Even the most basic steps of bringing your horse in from the field, grooming him and tacking up provide opportunities for the two of you to connect, assess each other's mood, and prepare yourselves physically and mentally for whatever it is you want to do – or, if necessary, revise your plans.

Many years ago I worked in a riding school. A pony called Adrian was sent to us for re-schooling. Adrian's infamy preceded him: he could buck for Britain! My colleague Lucy took on the heroic task. First she couldn't get anywhere near Adrian; she had to drive him into a little corral. Then she couldn't get a halter on him; it took two people to dodge his heels and get to his head. Then she couldn't groom him – he hated being touched and flinched from the brush. Then she couldn't tack him up – he jumped away from the saddle and girth and stuck his head in the air so she couldn't get the bridle on. Then he wouldn't stand still by the mounting block; she had to trap him against the wall and leap on board like a stunt rider. Then she couldn't stay on: he bucked until she fell off. She bravely persevered with this sequence for several weeks until the final fall sent her to hospital with a broken shoulder. Top marks for courage and tenacity – but wouldn't it have been even better to have listened to the pony, who was shouting 'No' loud and clear right from the start of the process?

(There's a happy ending to this story: Lucy made a full recovery; however her injury prompted Adrian's owner to find another home for him. Some good karma ripened for him: he went to a woman who listened to him. It took several years of relationship-building before Andie eventually managed to ride him, and then it was rather unconventional. She would wait for him to invite her up, which he would do by standing beside a log in the field and looking at her meaningfully. With nothing to restrain Adrian – not even a halter – Andie would climb onto the log and then onto the pony's back and the two of them would tootle off for a ride. When Adrian got fed up with it, he would stop and she would hop off and they'd walk home. Riding like this wouldn't suit everyone – and trying to do it could even be dangerous – but it worked for Adrian and Andie.)

Warming up the rider

Let's think of some of the main qualities you need to have as a rider. You need to be physically flexible, with good core strength. You need a good sense of balance, and of proprioception, meaning you know where each part of your body is and what it's doing. (This is more difficult than you might think; I have a left foot with a mind of its own – I need people to tell me when it's sticking out like a left-turn direction indicator!) You need to be calm, alert, focused, fully present and aware of what's going on with yourself, your horse, and the surrounding environment. You need to know what you want to do at all times so you can communicate your intention clearly to your horse. Perhaps we should stop here; that's plenty to start with. It's certainly enough to indicate the importance of some kind of ongoing fitness regime for body and mind, including practices like Pilates, Alexander Technique, yoga and meditation. It's also enough to indicate some useful warm-up exercises you can do before getting on your horse.

Leg stretches will loosen your hips and lower back, so you can sit flexibly in the saddle, moving with the horse – rather than perching lumpily on top and blocking his movement. Knee and ankle bends are also important. And remember your top half – loosen your shoulders, swing your arms, stretch your neck, move your jaw and wiggle your ears (if only to remind you of just one of the many ways in which your horse is your superior!).

Jumping about on the spot has a dual function: it gets your blood moving on winter days when you're cold and stiff, and it entertains your horse.

Standing on one leg with your eyes closed might look mad to any spectators, but it's great for improving your balance and proprioception. Closing your eyes for a moment also helps to bring your attention inwards, so you can become aware of how you're feeling and how you're breathing and where your energy is in your body. Breathe down into your tummy, and lower your centre of energy down to your hara or belly area.

If you find this last tip a bit mystifying, try this: if you could point to where you feel most alive in your body, where would you point? Where you point to indicates where your energy is most active at that moment. There's no need to get mystical about 'energy'. If you're interested in yogic things like prana and chakras, that's great; if not, that's great too. Martial arts make use of the energy in the hara, also called the tandien, which is an area inside the abdomen. Becoming aware of sensation in the belly will activate the energy in the hara, which is useful for being around horses, riding, and life in general. Horses are sensitive to how you use your energy: you can draw a horse towards you, or move him away, or influence him at a distance, by using the energy of your hara. Having your centre of energy down in the hara makes you stronger and more stable, meaning that you're less likely to be knocked over or pulled about when on the ground, and more likely to stay on the horse's back in a crisis when riding. If you want to experiment with these ideas, ask your horse to help you: he is an expert in energy awareness, and his responses will give you feedback as to how you're doing.

Moving on with our warm-up, if you're feeling anxious or agitated, don't deny it. Remember, you can't hide your feelings from your horse – but you can unsettle him by trying to deceive him. Talk to your horse about how you feel. If you're anxious and you want him to be calm and steady, say so. Or if you're keyed up and you want him to be similarly on his toes to jump some big fences, tell him how you feel and what you want.

Perhaps the most important point is that you need to be mentally switched on. Horses require us to be mentally present at all times, and can be quick to call us to order, perhaps by shying, if we're inattentive. Being aware of your body, your emotions, your breathing and your energy will help to bring your mind into the present moment. Your horse is naturally always in the here and now, ready to meet you when you arrive.

Warming up the horse

Now let's think of the qualities your horse needs to have for you to be able to enjoy riding him. He needs to be relaxed in body and mind, physically well-balanced, supple and able to move easily, attentive and responsive to the rider, cheerful, confident and co-operative.

Just as a human athlete benefits from training both mentally and physically, so can your horse benefit from building up his mental and physical fitness and flexibility. It's not a matter of your 'fixing' the horse as though there were something wrong with him, more a matter of your learning how to interact with him in such a way as to inspire and allow him to manifest his magnificence. Many riding and training problems are due to the human's obstructing the horse's natural perfection. Good training for horses is like yoga, promoting well-being on the physical, mental and spiritual levels so that the innate magnificence can shine out unobscured. It can take years of steady, correct practice for him to build up the physical fitness that will allow him to move with maximum ease and efficiency; it can also require a lot of mileage for him to gain the experience he needs in order to become a reliable riding horse, able to respond to the rider's requests and to handle with aplomb all the hazards he encounters.

Horses are physically very able – they are strong, fast, agile and capable of moving with grace and accuracy. They are also great dancers! Warming up the horse is an opportunity to encourage him to enjoy his ability to move. Aggressive methods and forceful gadgets, such as tight nosebands and restrictive reins, will inhibit his enthusiasm; it's much better to inspire and encourage him to take delight in his own natural ability.

Warming up your horse before you get on might include some or all of the following exercises:

❖ leading him about and moving him around with the tack on;

❖ loose schooling or lungeing gently for a couple of minutes at walk and trot, and maybe just one round of canter on each rein, to loosen him up and let him carry the saddle comfortably on his back;

❖ in-hand exercises, such as shoulder-in and leg-yield, to relax his jaw, flex his poll, stretch his neck, and encourage the inside hind leg to step up beneath him.

Relaxation and focus

We've already touched on the importance of relaxation, the first of the six scales of training (the others being rhythm, contact, straightness, impulsion and collection). It's the first of the six scales because you need it for all the others. It refers to an absence of stiffness or 'brace' in body and mind, and, although this is often forgotten, it applies as much to the rider as to the horse.

Relaxation is not laziness or sluggishness – it's quite the opposite. True relaxation frees the energy that would otherwise have been tied up in tension and resistance, and allows body and mind to move easily with fluidity, suppleness and grace.

Relaxation and focus go together. From the horse's point of view, both require him to have confidence in the rider's ability to keep everybody safe. Focus for horses normally means being fully in the present moment, with the attention scanning the environment and occasionally briefly zeroing in on one object. You can get some idea of it, now, if you momentarily quieten your internal mental chatter and relax your eyes to become aware of your peripheral vision: notice how your attention comes into the present moment, and spreads out around you. When we ride, we require the horse to withdraw his focus away from his surroundings, so he can be attentive to us and responsive to our aids. This new way of focusing takes practice to develop; it's very tiring at first, and young or unschooled horses get mentally exhausted easily. It's extremely important to keep schooling sessions short, to allow for frequent breaks during the session, and to notice the moment when the horse begins to tire so you can stop the session before he becomes exhausted.

A forceful rider can scare a horse into focusing on her, but she will never get relaxation that way. Shouting, 'You must relax!' while threatening someone with violence doesn't work! For relaxation as well as focus, the horse requires a genuinely trustworthy leader, not a bully. Remember, too, that it can be frightening for a horse to have a human staring at him; maybe he feels as though he's being assessed as a potential meal! A lot of lungeing problems come from this – the human stares at the horse, who gets scared and either goes faster in an attempt to get away from the threat or stops and turns to face it. He'll probably get used to it eventually, and learn to tolerate it – but why not be more considerate in the first place?

There are several good ways to encourage your horse to relax and focus; you can use them as a routine part of the warm-up and also whenever you need to refresh his relaxation and focus during your activities.

First off, set a good example. It's no good expecting your horse to be relaxed and focused if you're tense and distracted. Horses are very receptive to the influence of a leader they like and trust. So you need to demonstrate the way you want him to be.

Next, if you can encourage him to relax his jaw, you can go a long way towards relaxing the whole horse, body and mind. This is where a bit can be helpful. An increasing number of people nowadays are not using bits; they are riding in bitless bridles or even without bridles.. But if you learn how to use it to help the horse relax his jaw, you'll find that he will welcome the bit, looking forward to the pleasant experience it brings; we'll be looking at a simple way to do this in the Practice section at the end of this chapter. Of course you need to make sure the bit is comfortable, the correct width for his mouth, not too thick, and placed at the right height. Any noseband needs to be loose enough to allow him to move his jaw and tongue to interact conversationally with the bit; personally I prefer not to use a noseband at all – the less clutter on the horse's face, the better. It shouldn't need saying that any clumsy or harsh use of the bit will damage the horse's trust in you and prevent the relaxation you're seeking.

Combining relaxing the jaw with some lateral steps, such as leg-yield or shoulder-in, whether in-hand or ridden, is a marvellous exercise. Classical riding instructor Perry Wood describes the shoulder-in as being 'like the keys to a Ferrari.' These lateral steps can be introduced as early as you like – even before backing a young horse. They are so fabulous! Your horse will develop relaxation, focus and suppleness; he will learn to respond to your intention, and to the whisper of an aid; he will gain greater awareness of how he is moving and where he is placing his feet; and he will naturally, effortlessly, improve in balance and self-carriage and start to collect himself. What's not to like? In addition, if your horse were ever to become anxious or over-excited, a few steps of shoulder-in would have an instantly calming effect. Bending his body and giving him something interesting to do reclaims his focus and relaxes him: if he's revving up for take-off, the magical shoulder-in will steady him.

Relaxing the jaw combined with lateral steps, whether in-hand or ridden, offers an easy route to the wonderful, ecstatic experience of 'floating'. This occurs when there is a complete absence of 'brace' or resistance in the body and mind of both horse and human; the two of you are moving as one, dancing together. A horse who is floating with his human partner has a joyful expression on his face, with soft and shining eyes; he looks as though he is smiling. The human looks much the same! Humans describe it in various ways, my favourite being 'all the cells in my body are smiling', which is a description that I think would probably work for the horse too. 'Floating' takes us into the territory of the centaur-experience previously mentioned; it's really quite accessible, and the more you practise it, the more accessible it becomes.

Let's turn now to some practical exercises you can do with your horse as part of your preparation for riding.

PRACTICE

We're going to do two practical exercises: relaxing the horse's jaw with the bit, and shoulder-in in hand. Your horse needs to be wearing a comfortable snaffle bridle with no noseband. You'll need a long stick; a dressage whip is ideal, or a long twig picked from the hedge. Hazel twigs are traditionally used in classical riding, the only drawback being that you can go through several twigs per session as your horse enjoys the nibbles so thoughtfully provided!

Remember to apply whatever you've learned that might be relevant as you do these exercises, for example making sure that you're in a calm, alert state of mind, with a friendly attitude. You might like to make a circle of excellence for yourself and your horse to help you both to be 'in the zone'.

You could also usefully remind yourself of the six coaching elements of any practice session: Purpose, Intention, Preparation, Activity, Reflection, and Enjoyment.

RELAXING THE JAW WITH THE BIT

❖   Start by standing politely alongside the horse,
      facing the same way
       – so you're not staring straight at him, but you

can see his jaw and the side of his head.

❖ Take a very gentle contact with the rein nearest to you. I remember being taught as a child to hold the reins with the sort of delicacy that would be needed to hold a tiny bird. Imagine the rein is a little bird: it's alive in your hand and you can feel its breathing and its heartbeat. You need to hold it gently, and also sufficiently positively that it can feel safe, so it doesn't panic and try to escape.

❖ Your hand should be held quite high relative to the bit. It is more comfortable for the horse to 'converse' with a higher contact than with a lower one. Backwards or downwards pressure causes the bit to press on the tongue and the bars of the jaw, and also, with a jointed bit that bends in the middle, to push up into the roof of the mouth. These pressures prompt the horse to open his jaw to alleviate the pain or discomfort; many riders deal with this problem, not by changing what they are doing, but simply strapping the jaw shut with a tight noseband.

❖ Now start conversing with the horse by moving your fingers on the rein. Try gently wiggling or feathering the fingers, or slightly squeezing them.

❖ As soon as he responds by moving his jaw and relaxing it – which you will be able to both see and feel – let your fingers be softly still, while remaining very alive and aware and in touch with his mouth via the rein.

❖ Praise your horse verbally as soon as he makes any attempt to respond to your requests, so he knows that you're appreciating his efforts. Encourage him by telling him that he's doing well, and that he's a clever and magnificent horse.

❖ Do the same exercise on the other side, with the other rein.

❖ Now add to the exercise by inviting the jaw to relax, and then – very gently – inviting the horse to turn his head to the side, towards you, so he bends his neck. Make sure you are standing in a position that gives him room to do this. He will naturally lower his head and flex his poll as he turns his head towards you. Again, do this on both sides.

This exercise gives you an excellent opportunity to increase your sensitivity to communication from your horse. Being careful to avoid staring at him, you can be lovingly aware of his facial expression, particularly the expression in his eye. Notice when his face goes smooth and his eye softens and he seems to smile. Notice also whether or not there is any brace or resistance as he responds to your invitation to turn his head by bending his neck and flexing at the poll. Be aware of the moment when the brace disappears, and your horse is just purely, trustingly accepting your invitation. Notice how this occurs when you and he are mentally tuned in to each other, your minds meeting in the present moment, both focused on what you're doing together. This is not just a physical exercise – it's a meditation practice. And this what is meant by 'relaxation and focus'.

Don't go on for too long with this jaw-relaxing exercise – just do it a couple of times each way and then take a break for reflection before doing something else.

SHOULDER-IN IN HAND

There are some preliminaries you may need to establish before practising the shoulder-in.

❖ Take a while to ensure that your horse is comfortable with your stroking him with the stick and waving it around over his head and body. He must be able to trust that you are not going to hit him. You also need to give him time to discern your intention. As long as you have no intention for him to respond, he needn't take any notice of the stick; however, when you do intend him to respond, just the tiniest twitch or lightest touch of it is significant and requires his attention.

❖ You need to be sure that you can move his shoulder away from you. It's difficult to do in-hand exercises if your horse has any tendency to shove you with his shoulder. Stand beside him, level with his shoulder, facing towards him. You want him to move his forehand a step or two away from you; you're going to ask him for a step or two of a turn on the haunches. With your energy down in the hara, you breathe out while looking where you want him to go (which means looking through him as though he were transparent) as you use both hands to touch his shoulder and neck, or, sometimes, the side of his head. (You may like to revisit the Who moves who? exercise in Chapter Five. Moving the forehand away is an easy next step after those four basic moves.)

❖ You're nearly ready for the shoulder-in! You just need to familiarise yourself and your horse with the basic in-hand position. We'll start on the nearside.

❖ Stand alongside your horse, level with his left shoulder and facing towards him. The reins are resting on the horse's neck as though ready for a rider.

❖ Take the left rein gently in your left hand, a couple of inches from the bit. Remember to keep the left hand fairly high, as that will be more comfortable for your horse.

❖ The right hand has to multi-task, holding both the right rein and also the stick. Turn the right hand so it is palm up, and hold the stick alongside the horse so you can easily touch his side and quarters. Now take hold of the right rein, probably somewhere near the central buckle, and gently take a very light contact with it. This rein is going lie against the right side of the horse's neck and support the left rein.

❖ Pause for a moment to make sure you've got your hands and the reins and the stick all sorted out, and remember to breathe.

❖ Reassure your horse that it will all work out fine and it's going to be fun – honestly!

❖ Now turn your body slightly to the front, and ask your horse to walk on. You'll need to relax the

rein contact fractionally to allow him to move.
You may need to touch him with the stick to
encourage him forward.

❖ Set the pace yourself; he must match you. You
want a slow, measured walk, called a 'school walk',
that gives both of you time to think about what
you're doing.

❖ Just walk slowly around together for a while like
this, experimenting with how you need to turn
your body and use your energy and manage your
own walking steps to set the slow pace and steady
rhythm that suits you. Practise starting, stopping
and turning in each direction. Encourage your
horse with praise as you go along.

❖ Have a break, and congratulate both your horse
and yourself. You can both reassure yourselves
that this will become easy with practice.

❖ Now do it again, from the other side.

❖ Take another break.

Now for the shoulder-in (or shoulder-fore, which is a very gentle,
beginning sort of shoulder-in). As the name implies, shoulder-in is an
exercise in which the horse's shoulders are brought inwards off the
track along which he is travelling. You are going to ask him to walk
slowly along a straight line; then, with his hind quarters continuing to
follow that track, you are going to invite him to relax his jaw and bring
his head slightly in towards you as he walks slowly along, and, in
addition, to bring his shoulders slightly to the inside, towards you. This
will mean that he is travelling forward along the original straight line (it's

easiest if you do this exercise alongside a fence), with his front end slightly to the inside. His inside hind leg will be stepping up and under his body more, but otherwise his hindquarters are unchanged.

So off you go. (These instructions are for when you're on his near side.)

❖   Establish your position, and ask him to walk forward slowly and steadily. You set the pace and tempo, and he matches you.

❖   As you walk slowly alongside the fence, use the fingers of your left hand to invite him to relax his jaw and bring his head slightly towards you. You will need to position yourself a little further away from him to allow him the space to do this.

❖   With your right hand, keep the stick by his side, ready to keep his hindquarters alongside the fence.

❖   Your multi-tasking right hand will keep the contact with the right rein. This right rein will lie against his neck, and as you step slightly away from him, drawing his shoulder slightly towards you, it will both support that invitation and also control the amount he bends his neck.

❖   Remember to breathe, and to praise your clever, clever horse, who is now walking along in a perfect shoulder-in. Notice how happy he looks – his jaw is soft, his eye is soft and he is smiling. Horses love shoulder-in. It feels wonderful!

❖   Stop and praise him some more. Give him a treat

and tell him he is marvellous!

❖ Reflect on what's gone on and how you might improve.

❖ Do the exercise from the other side. It's usually easier on one side than the other. If your horse makes heavy weather of it in one direction, he is not being naughty – he is struggling with a physical unevenness, in just the same way as I bet you would find it harder to sit in the full lotus posture one way than the other. Just as your yoga teacher would gently support you with practising the posture repeatedly over a period of many months, until you become equally strong and flexible, so you can gently support your horse likewise with the shoulder-in and other exercises.

As you and your horse gain familiarity with the shoulder-in, it will become easier and more beautiful, and you will share the blissful floating experience, when the two of you are moving in total harmony, the reins delightfully light, with no trace of a brace in either of you.

Remember that it is tiring for your horse to focus in this way, so keep the in-hand sessions very short, with lots of breaks. The shoulder-in exercise is supposed to be delightful, so be careful you don't discourage him by overdoing it and exhausting him. Let his physical and mental strength develop gradually.

You can see how practising in-hand exercises such as shoulder-in for a few minutes before you ride will help both you and your horse to warm up mentally and physically and establish the relaxation and focus you need for enjoyable riding.

CHAPTER TEN:

RIDING

So now you and your horse are all warmed up and ready to go. But before you jump on there's one more thing to consider, which is that it's a privilege to ride a horse, not a right. Any horse can ditch any rider at any time. Rodeo riders stay on board for a matter of seconds before they come off – and they are the experts. Your horse must be willing to allow you to ride him; we saw in the cautionary tale of Adrian what can happen if he isn't. So let's think about what might need to be in it for him.

Why would your horse want to be ridden?

Companionship is one possibility. Horses enjoy being with their friends. A horse with a human friend probably finds the human rather limiting. She's very slow and she gets tired easily – it's simply easier to carry her!

Security might be another benefit. Just as you might feel safer walking in the woods at night with a big dog to protect you, so your horse probably feels safer with a trustworthy human to encourage and protect him.

Personal development is a third possibility. This might sound fanciful, but it isn't. Horses enjoy the feeling of well-being that good riding brings them. Once a horse realises how a good schooling session enables him to feel wonderful, he becomes interested in the process and his enthusiasm increases so that he welcomes the rider and is eager to practise.

All these benefits are included and exceeded in the centaur experience, which requires the participation of both a horse and a human, and which some horses will actively seek to bring about. This occurs when the horse and rider are so deeply connected, physically, mentally and spiritually, that together they become something greater than the totality of two separate beings. It can be described as experiencing a sense of connection with the universe, or the web of being, or interdependence or whatever you want to call it. Just a glimpse of this ecstatic, uplifting experience will enchant you and your horse and keep you both coming back for more.

For any of these possibilities to apply, mutual trust is necessary. This is why it's so important to question some common practices, such as training approaches based on correction. We've already seen that some traditional concepts need re-thinking, such as 'catching' your horse. The whip is another one to rethink. Some people prefer to call it a stick; others use the word 'wand'. Whatever you call it, it's an extension of your arm, to assist communication, not a means of punishment.

As I said, trust needs to be mutual. If you don't trust your horse – you're afraid that he doesn't always wish you well, and that he might buck or take off with you – take your fears seriously. They may be accurate. If you're worried about your horse you may need to get help to improve your relationship. You may even need to re-home the horse, who might get on better with somebody else, and look for a more suitable horse for yourself.

Getting on

Having decided that it's OK to get on, it's best to use a mounting block
of some kind; a fence or gate will do. The less you have to disturb the
saddle and pull on the horse's back, the better. Ask your horse's
permission to get on. If he moves away from the mounting block, don't
assume he's being naughty. He may be trying to tell you that he's
worried about your getting on because his back hurts, or his saddle
pinches, or you stick your toe in his side or thump into the saddle when
you mount, or the last time you rode him you grabbed at the reins and
it damn well hurt and he doesn't want to risk that again. He may be
more relaxed if you turn him around so he's facing the other way. In
the classical story of Alexander the Great and Bucephalus, it's said that
Alexander turned the frightened horse to face the sun so he couldn't
be spooked by his own shadow. Then Alexander was able to jump on,
and the pair galloped off to conquer most of Asia! If your horse is
happy for you to get on, he'll stand by the mounting block and invite
you up. Your good manners in waiting to be invited will be good for
your relationship – and greatly increase your chances of remaining safely
in the saddle.

   A client of mine, Carla, had a big half-bred mare called Florence,
who wouldn't stand still for the rider to get on. Carla checked
everything carefully – back, teeth and all the tack. It all seemed fine.
Still Florence was fidgeting so badly that the only way up was by means
of a leap worthy of a stunt rider. She would also refuse to stand still
while out on a ride, which was a problem on our narrow Exmoor lanes,
where you often have to wait in a lay-by for a vehicle to pass. I thought
it worth experimenting with clicker training; if Florence didn't respond
quickly to treats, then Carla would need to do more detective work,
but if she did, maybe that would solve the problem. I showed Carla
how to click and treat Florence when she stood still, and to stay calm,
without clicking or treating, when she fidgeted. A few weeks later
Carla rang me. She started off with, 'I have a complaint to make...' and
I thought, 'Oh dear' – but she continued, laughing, 'Now when I get on,

Florence won't move until I've given her a treat. And then she stops in every lay-by we come to and turns her head to ask for a treat. I have to take lots of carrots with me whenever I ride!' I took that as a good result.

So now you're on board, let's get on with riding! This brings me to a slightly tricky point. In my work with clients I come across many people who have crucial gaps in their knowledge of how to ride, or have received wrong information. For example, students are commonly instructed to ride with a contact (often with short reins so their arms are sticking out in front of them) before they have developed a secure seat. And many people tell me they have been instructed to pull on the reins to put the horse on the bit. Aagh! This is not a riding instruction manual, so, apart from instructions for the specific practical exercises, I can't include general riding instructions. However you'll find some good riding manuals listed in the reading section at the end of the book and I urge you to explore them: the better you ride, the more you and your horse will enjoy yourselves.

Schooling

People often complain that schooling is boring. They're right – if you don't know what to do, and you just sort of trot about, it's extremely boring. But if you have a purpose, so you know why you're doing it, along with some ideas of what to do and how to do it, then schooling can be interesting and enjoyable, even exciting, exhilarating, ecstatic and utterly enchanting!

If you don't have a proper arena, don't despair. Just a few years ago hardly anyone had an arena; we all rode in fields. To have a flat field relatively free of lumps, bumps, stones and trees with low branches was a luxury. It's helpful to mark out your riding area with portable dressage markers to give your riding a kind of geographical focus, which is a great psychological support. If you like, you can temporarily enclose the area with push-in fencing posts and tape. (Your horse may be wary of the tape if he has any experience of electric fencing, so be sure to introduce him to it carefully so he knows he won't get a shock if he touches it.)

We're going to run through some points that are useful to remember when coaching yourself for riding. You could write down those you find especially useful on a piece of paper to carry with you and refer to during your breaks. It's also good if you can get somebody else to read them out to you as you're riding. Also, although the aim is for the mind to be calm, aware and fully present, most people have some ongoing mental chatter, and you can use this inner self-talk constructively to remind yourself of useful points. This list is just a start; you'll be able to add your own points to it.

❖ Remember the six coaching elements: Purpose, Intention, Preparation, Action, Reflection and Enjoyment, which apply to the entire practice session and to each activity within the session.

❖ Remember that less is more: the less you do, the better. Don't over-ride. Sit quietly, ask gently, and let the horse do it.

❖ Remember to Invite, Allow, and Enjoy.

❖ Remember to encourage your horse – and yourself – with praise as you go along. Don't wait until you've stopped to praise him, or he'll think that stopping is the clever bit. Treats are very encouraging too.

❖ Remember to breathe, to smile, to relax and to keep your energy low in your hara area.

❖ Remember to communicate in stages: a thought, a

whisper, a nudge, a tap. If he still doesn't respond, experiment to find out what works better – and look out for how you might be blocking him.

❖ Remember to let your horse be your coach: he may not be doing what you want, but he might well be doing what you're asking. He is probably going exactly in accordance with the way you are riding him. Respect his feedback and ask yourself what you can learn from it.

❖ Remember to have frequent breaks during your schooling session. More than just physical and mental rests, breaks allow you both to assimilate what you're learning, which speeds up the learning process.

❖ Remember to play, be creative, enjoy yourself and share your enjoyment with your horse.

❖ Remember to appreciate your horse's willing co-operation.

The above coaching points can apply at all times, whatever you're doing. Let's look now at some specific practical riding exercises.

PRACTICE

VISUALISATION

Make a circle of excellence that includes both of you, then develop that by imagining a coloured line extending from the circle out in front of you. Alter the colour of the line at the places where you want to change the gait or to change the pace within the gait. For example, brighten the colour to energise or speed up the pace, or soften the colour to steady or slow down the pace; change to a different colour for a change of gait; and stop the line where you want to halt. (You might like to refer to Chapters 4 and 5 to refresh your memory for this exercise.)

CONTACT

You don't need tight or even taut reins for contact; your horse can feel you when the reins are quite long or even loose. Try this experiment. While he is standing still with you on his back, pick up the reins, keeping them slack. Now experiment with tightening and relaxing your grip, wiggling your fingers, and moving your hand position, all while keeping the reins slack. Notice your horse's responses. He can feel what you are doing even with loose reins (unless of course he has gone to sleep). And later on, when you've finished riding and are relaxing at home, you can inspire yourself by looking at videos of classical riders on YouTube, their horses collected in self-carriage, with the reins loose.

FEEL

Here's a little exercise to help you to ride with 'feel', which is sometimes called the holy grail of riders. 'Feel' refers to your awareness of what is going on with the horse and yourself in body and mind. It means knowing where each part of his body is at any moment, and how he is about to move, and your balance and position relative to this, and the precise moment at which to apply an aid so he can respond instantly and easily. Then you won't ask him to move his inside hind leg just when it is supporting his weight and he either has to hop, or delay responding until the next step: making that sort of mistake too often will annoy even the most tolerant of horses.

Developing feel requires you to have a quiet mind, undistracted by inner chatter. It needs practice, with attention paid to the feedback coming from the horse.

A simple starting point is this: as your horse is standing still, put your awareness in your seat, your bum. Either ask him to walk on, slowly, or have somebody lead him forward for you. Keeping your awareness in your bum, notice what you can feel. Later, as your awareness develops, try this in trot and canter. Notice your horse's response as you momentarily shift your awareness to your bum as you're trotting or cantering.

Experiment with timing your leg aids, one leg at a time, in synch with the swing of his belly as he moves, and in harmony with his foot falls. You need to ask him to move a particular leg at the moment when the foot is coming off the ground and is free to move.

If you can trust your horse to stay underneath you, and not shy or take off, try closing your eyes for brief periods to help you to focus on your feel. It might be safest to practise this at the walk, with someone leading the horse.

INVITE YOUR HORSE TO HELP YOU

It's a marvellous moment when you and your horse discover the delight of real partnership in riding, when you're helping each other to bring about more enjoyment for both of you. For your horse to have both the willingness and the confidence to offer to help without fear of being rebuffed or 'corrected', you as the rider must be trustworthy, with a co-operative, encouraging attitude. Try this experiment. When you're practising sitting trot, invite your horse to 'offer his back' for you to sit on. Ask for a slow trot, and sit lightly – mostly as an attitude of mind, but also with the slight physical component of your bum being just a fraction of a millimetre above the saddle. This invites your horse to lift his back, as he seeks the connection with your seat. Accept his raised back, sit softly on it, and hurray, you're now moving together, the sitting trot is flowing easily, and you're both feeling fabulous!

SHOULDER-IN

The more proficient you are with the shoulder-in in hand, the easier you'll find the shoulder-in under saddle. Here are some basic instructions for you to try; you might want to consult a good riding instruction manual for more detailed instructions.

- ❖ Walk slowly – a school walk – alongside the fence.

- ❖ Gently ask the horse to relax his jaw and turn his head slightly to the inside, by conversing with him via the fingers of your hand on the inside rein.

- ❖ Turn your body slightly to the inside, keeping the inside hip back, and the inside leg lightly against his side. This will indicate to the horse that he is not to walk off to the inside. (If you wanted him to actually turn in and walk on, you would advance the inside hip and loosen the inside leg.)

- ❖ Support with the outside rein against the neck, both to prevent too much bend, and to encourage the shoulders to move slightly to the inside. You may need to give a tiny little half halt on the outside rein, to steady the horse, encourage him to shift his weight off his shoulders, and make it even clearer that you don't want him to turn in and walk off to the inside.

- ❖ Keep your aids very light. This is definitely an

exercise in which the less you do, the better.
Don't be tempted to get stronger with your horse
if nothing is happening; just try again, gently. If
your horse insists on turning to the inside and
walking away from the fence line, check your own
balance. If you are sitting with your weight to the
inside, he is very kindly trying to stay underneath
you! You must keep your weight absolutely
central so he can continue along the fence.

Remember the benefits of shoulder-in – 'the keys to a Ferrari' – and
practise it often. You don't have to be schooling to do it – you can
easily do a few steps as you're riding along a track or lane. In the next
chapter, on Confidence Coaching, we'll see how useful the shoulder-in
is for managing equine nerves. Having such a marvellous resource for
managing an excited or frightened horse does wonders for the rider's
confidence.

CHAPTER ELEVEN:
CONFIDENCE COACHING

Any effective coaching is going to improve your confidence as a natural by-product of helping you to learn how to do something better. All the topics we've covered so far are relevant for improving confidence, and you've probably already noticed how much more confident you're feeling with the coaching skills you've already gained.

In this chapter we're going to look at some further suggestions specifically aimed at improving your confidence as a rider. We're also going to look at improving your horse's confidence. Your confidence and your horse's confidence are linked because if one of you is at ease, it helps the other to feel similarly relaxed – and vice versa.

Let's start by considering two very basic issues: firstly, why you might want to improve your confidence – and, secondly, why you might have reservations about doing so.

Why – and why not – improve your confidence?

Take a few minutes now to consider some of the possible benefits of your being more confident, with particular regard to your relationships with:

❖ your horse

❖ other people in your horsy context

❖ other people beyond your horsy context.

You might like to write a list of the benefits you can think of now, and keep it handy so you can add to it over time. Have some fun with your list and find some big bright benefits to motivate yourself.

The next thing is to address any reservations you might have about increasing your confidence. It might seem strange, but people are sometimes concerned about becoming too confident.

Reservations tend to fall into three main areas. First, nobody likes a smarty-pants, someone who's not just confident, but tiresomely cocky. Second, over-confident people tend to underestimate risks and are likely to make mistakes that endanger themselves and others. Third, some people are only confident because they don't know any better and their ignorance means they're oblivious to real dangers. So, if there's a part of you that shrinks from the idea of increasing your confidence, maybe it wants to protect you from becoming a risk-taking, ignorant smarty-pants! You need to reassure this genuinely helpful part of yourself that you can increase your confidence wisely, so you can expand the range of activities you enjoy doing while remaining a nice person who can assess risks accurately.

Fear

It's important to understand that confidence coaching isn't about eliminating fear. As we discussed in Chapter Four, there are different kinds of fear. There's a 'being on your toes' feeling when you're meeting a challenge; it's a kind of excitement, although it can seem very similar to fear. There's a chronic anxiety that many people live with every day, regardless of whether or not there's any actual danger. There's a healthy caution regarding any hazardous activity, based on a realistic assessment of risk. And there's the alarm that warns us of real danger. With the possible exception of chronic anxiety, all these kinds of fear are very useful in keeping us alive.

Some years ago I was asked to help a woman who had lost her nerve for hunting. She was deeply ashamed to admit that she had become afraid to gallop across unknown terrain. It turned out that she had had a terrible fall out hunting: while galloping over rough ground, her horse had put his foot in a hole and turned over and she had been catapulted off with great force and had broken her back. Part of her mind wanted someone to wave a wand and remove her fear so she could carry on careering about as before; but part of her mind was determined to stop her taking such crazy risks. Having explained that I wasn't prepared to try to help her overrule her fear, I encouraged her to see that this might be an opportunity to find other ways of enjoying her riding, and also, if she wanted to, to reflect on what she valued so much about hunting and to consider how she might find that fulfilment in other ways.

If you're seriously afraid for your safety with regard to your riding, please don't try to dismiss your fear or overrule it. It's trying to keep you alive! Pay particular attention to how you feel about your relationship with your horse. You must be able to trust each other's goodwill. If you think that your horse might not be not well-intentioned towards you, please get help. If the relationship doesn't improve, then re-home the horse. The risks of being around a horse who is careless of your well-being, or, worse, actually wants to hurt you, are very high.

Comfort zones

Our confidence levels naturally vary and fluctuate day-to-day. We have familiar comfort zones, areas of activity in which we feel confident, but these tend to shrink when we're feeling vulnerable due to being stressed, worried, unwell, tired, after a frightening experience or following a period of reduced activities. We've already seen that many women find their comfort zones temporarily diminishing with the arrival of children, and again during menopause. The good news is that comfort zones can be expanded. We can gently stretch them by repeatedly encouraging ourselves to go just a tiny bit further than is entirely comfortable. We can also encourage ourselves to become more at ease with uncertainty and spontaneity, and to enjoy the exhilaration of exciting activities.

Notice the word 'encouragement': en-*courage*-ment. Encouraging someone helps them to find the courage to do more than they thought they could. It's crucial to approach confidence issues with an encouraging attitude. There is no place for aggression or criticism towards yourself or your horse. You can't increase anyone's confidence by attacking them; that isn't coaching, it's bullying.

The spookability scale

We know that emotions are infectious, especially fear. This is a survival thing: as social beings, we need to know instantly if another member of our group is aware of danger. Sometimes the fear we feel when riding actually starts with our horse's fear. As prey animals, horses are predisposed to be alert to potential dangers and they are easily alarmed. Some horses seem to operate at a default level of unusually high alert; just walking along a quiet lane, their adrenalin is up around their ears, and they are radiating waves of anxiety. Riding such a horse feels like sitting on an active volcano that could erupt at any moment; the rider would have to be unconscious not to be scared in such a situation. And of course the process also works the other way: if a rider is apprehensive, the horse will pick it up and become fearful – which scares the rider even more.

I find the concept of a spookability scale helpful in relation to riding and horsemanship; it's a good conceptual tool for assessing where you and your horse are at any moment and also for measuring your progress. Think of a scale of 1 – 10, with 1 being peacefully asleep and 10 being total crazy panic. If your horse is walking along at level 4, a sparrow flying by will momentarily attract his attention, putting him up to level 5; then, having clocked that it's a sparrow, he'll revert to his normal level 4. But if he is already at level 8, the sparrow flying by will jolt him up to 9, and he'll shy. He can't help but do this – it's a reflex reaction that's too quick for conscious intervention. It's the lightning speed of this startle reaction that has kept horses alive on a planet full of predators for millions of years of evolution; ironically, it's the main factor making horses potentially dangerous to themselves and others in the modern world.

Some people talk about 'de-sensitising' horses to make them less reactive to scary things, but I prefer to think of lowering the settings on the spookability scale, combined with expanding the comfort zone. I don't think 'de-sensitised' is a good descriptive term to apply to a confident, relaxed, happy horse who is responsive to his rider – which is surely what you want.

The spookability scale applies to you too. If you're relaxed and alert, at maybe level 4 on the scale, a small surprise such as a bike coming round the corner will send you up to 5 or 6; then you'll realise that it's just a bike, and quickly recover your aplomb. But if you're already anxious, perhaps at 7, the appearance of the bike will send you up to 8 or 9, grabbing at the reins and alarming your horse – who might have been fine about the bike without your over-reaction.

When I started working with Martin and Chris, Martin's default level when being ridden was around level 8. He was almost oblivious to the rider, ignoring all known aids and refusing to go forward (although he could go backwards very fast indeed). Various well-meaning people had diagnosed him as naughty and nappy and had applied whips and spurs to try to make him go forward, so he had shut down to protect himself from the pain. He would stand with his feet planted, as though paralysed with fear; then a leaf would rustle and he would erupt from a standstill into a flat-out gallop and bolt for home. Hardly surprisingly, Chris's default level was also an 8, as she crouched in the saddle in the classic foetal position of extreme fear, clutching at the reins with a white-knuckled grip about a foot from the bit. It was impossible to do anything with them both in that state. Hence our starting again, with stroking, grooming, leading, liberty practice, clicker training and play, to repair their relationship, re-establish their communication and get both of them down to a default level of 4 on the scale. They both needed re-sensitising, not de-sensitising: they had to re-awaken their sensitivity in order to be able to communicate with each other. From being oblivious to the aids, Martin gradually opened up to respond to a thought, a whisper, a breath, a touch. Chris gradually learned to relax, breathe, sit up and lengthen her reins. With better communication in both directions, Chris could notice as soon as Martin began to get worried, and could reassure him immediately instead of letting his fear increase to take-off point. And as Martin's trust in humans developed, and his relationship with Chris improved, so he began to see the rider as a source of support and encouragement rather than another threat in a hostile world.

Relationship

Much of my work with horses and riders consists of operating a kind of equestrian 'Relate' relationship counselling service. Horse and rider need to be able to trust each other; if either is scared of the other, then he or she will inevitably be elevated on the spookability scale with predictably unfortunate results.

As we've seen throughout this book, relationship-building takes place at every encounter, not just riding. Non-riding activities like horse agility, liberty play, doing tricks and just hanging out with your horse are all great for improving your relationship.

Clicker training can be very helpful to increase your horse's confidence. It is still the case that many horses are trained largely through correction, inhibiting unwanted behaviour (this can of course be done with varying degrees of skill, and doesn't necessarily mean punishment). The beauty of clicker training is that the horse is encouraged to experiment with doing things differently, to get the human to produce a treat. There's an element of role-reversal, in that the horse takes the initiative in working out for himself what he needs to do to get the human to respond in the right way. It's wonderful to see an inhibited horse start to perk up and enjoy himself as he is encouraged to take an active part in training sessions. It's fun for the horse to train a human to hand out treats!

Spooky horses respond well to clicker training, as objects that would previously have been viewed as scary monsters are transformed into treat opportunities. Instead of retreating or shying away from the menacing dustbin, the horse advances bravely towards it, confident that touching it with his nose will bring praise and treats. Every such incident improves your relationship, as he learns that you can be trusted: if you say something is safe, then it really is safe. Conversely, punishing him for shying damages your relationship as it demonstrates your untrustworthiness, sending him rocketing up the spookability scale and increasing the likelihood of his shying again.

Riders need to understand their horses' aptitude for generalising. This, along with the lightning fast startle reaction, is another survival strategy: a wild horse who discovers that one large rock provides cover for a predator realises that he must beware of all large rocks – and bushes, trees, logs and other miscellaneous objects – from then on. Failure to generalise from the one incident could result in his becoming somebody's lunch in the future. The equine propensity to generalise means that riders unwittingly make matters worse by punishing horses for shying, thereby turning a trivial incident into a major one. The horse generalises from the unpleasant experience – and the rider has created an ongoing problem. Patience and good humour on the part of the rider in the first place would have given the horse the confidence to expand his comfort zone, thereby reducing his tendency to shy in the future.

Focus

Your horse's attention is naturally temporally focused, in the sense of being in the present moment rather than day-dreaming about the past or future, but is normally spatially diffuse as he is scanning the surrounding environment for possible dangers. The more you can encourage him to focus on you, and on the interaction taking place between the two of you, the safer he is to handle or ride. It takes time to increase his ability to do this and at first he will only be able to sustain this focus for short periods before getting tired. It's rather like you learning to meditate: in the beginning you can only focus for a minute or two, but with practice you can gradually lengthen the periods. There's an additional factor for your horse: he needs you to demonstrate your ability to keep him safe, so he no longer feels compelled to look out for danger. This is where strong, trustworthy, capable leadership is important.

Horses vary in their ability to focus on their riders. Arabs, as a breed, have a reputation for flightiness. They tend to be very alert and interested in what's going on in their environment; they are also very intelligent, and it can be a challenge to engage their interest enough to get them to focus on you. In addition, research has shown that Arabs have a longer flight distance than most horses, meaning that if they take off they run further before stopping. Stallions can also present a focusing challenge, as can individuals who are accustomed to taking a lead role in the herd and therefore are strongly predisposed to be on the look-out for danger in order to keep everybody safe.

Firmness

As a rider, in addition to being encouraging and good-humoured you will also need to be a firm, no-nonsense leader when necessary. It's natural for your horse to test your leadership; from his point of view his life could depend on you and he wants evidence that you're up to the job of keeping him safe. So you need to know what you're doing and what you want, or he is likely to take matters into his own hooves. You must be prepared to mean business, set clear boundaries and insist on the standards of behaviour that you require. Good manners are non-negotiable! This applies to you too: if you want your horse to be polite, you need to demonstrate what you want. This means developing your ability to be courteous as well as clear and firm. Your consistency in these things will enable your horse to know where he is and what's required of him, so that he can feel that he's in safe hands. Then you'll both feel calmer and safer around each other.

Of course, if you don't know what you're doing or what you want, you must be honest about it. Trying to deceive your horse will only make matters worse. If you need help, get it! Don't just struggle on alone, hoping that things will work out; the risks are too great. Having an unmanageable horse is not like having a badly-behaved bunny. The bunny may be annoying; the horse may be dangerous.

Don't shoot the messenger

Having said this about the need to be firm, and to know what you're doing, I appreciate that this is often exactly where the problem lies: we don't always know what we're doing with our horse, and, even if we recognise that firmness is required, we don't know how to be firm without being horrible. Other people, often with good intentions, may be advising us to use physical violence such as hitting the horse or applying harsh bits and tight nosebands and other gadgets. We find ourselves feeling confused and unhappy – and no nearer to resolving our issues with our similarly confused and unhappy horse.

In such a situation it's important to pause and take a deep breath. Ask yourself what your horse is trying to communicate, and what needs to be different for him to be OK with whatever it is you want him to do. In considering these questions, there are two factors that are often overlooked: the significance of environment, and the equine capacity for empathy.

I once kept my two horses at a livery yard over the winter. As time went on they became increasingly unmanageable, to the point where I was warning people to keep clear of their heels because my normally gentle horses were so upset they were likely to kick! Riding them became impossible – they were too wild to get on. The atmosphere at this yard was horrible, with distress and anger emanating both from the humans running the place and from unhappy, neglected horses who were stabled there. My horses were picking up the distress and anger and expressing it themselves. As soon as we moved to a place with a happier atmosphere they regained their usual cheerfulness.

The horse's propensity to pick up and express others' emotions is also relevant with regard to his rider. I often find that horses who are reluctant to do something, such as hacking out, are actually expressing the rider's issue. The rider is unsure about hacking out, and the horse is manifesting the human's doubts. Clearly it is not only ineffective but also unjust and cruel to 'shoot the messenger' by punishing the horse in such cases.

Talking of confidence issues with regard to hacking, I want to fly the flag for hackers everywhere! If your main activity is hacking, don't let anyone patronise you or criticise you for it. Hacking requires courage and resourcefulness in both horse and rider to deal with an unpredictable, uncontrollable environment full of hazards such as vehicles whirling round blind corners on the roads and mountain bikes speeding along the bridleways. And you know what? Many of those super-duper competitive riders who sneer at 'happy hackers' don't dare to venture outside the safety of a riding arena or show ring. They're in no position to get on their high horses and look down their noses at people who enjoy hacking!

Key coaching questions

As we've seen throughout this book, asking good questions is one of the keys to effective coaching. This applies to confidence issues as much as to anything else.

Perhaps the first question to ask yourself is this: *What needs to be different for me to feel more confident?*

According to your own specific context, the question can be applied with regard to your environment, your horse, the people around you, and to yourself personally. Ask yourself the question repeatedly, to come up with several answers. Possible answers might include setting more realistic goals, improving your skills by having riding lessons, getting help with training your horse, riding at a different time of day in order to avoid heavy traffic, finding a suitable riding companion, moving to a friendlier livery yard, and turning your horse out before riding so he has a chance to let off steam without you on his back.

When you have several ideas in mind, take a few minutes to imagine yourself in some possible future scenarios with the changes in place and notice which changes have the greatest effect on how you feel.

You can also apply this question to your horse: *What needs to be different for him to feel more confident?* If your horse could answer, what might he say? Perhaps he would appreciate different management in terms of turnout, tack, feed, foot care, handling or companionship. Would he like to be ridden more positively and effectively, so he can have more confidence in his rider? Would he benefit from more time spent introducing him to scary objects, maybe with the help of clicker training? Perhaps he would welcome a magnesium supplement to calm his nerves; magnesium deficiency, which causes horses to be nervous and jumpy, can occur in areas where the soil is deficient in magnesium (it's common here on Exmoor).

Thinking about what your horse might be trying to tell you can have a big impact on your relationship with him. Do your best to understand what your horse is communicating: it's not realistic to expect him to see things from your point of view – it's up to you to empathise with his point of view.

Another good coaching question to ask yourself is: *What could I learn from this experience (or situation, issue or incident), if I wanted to?* You can apply this question whether things are going well, or not so well. Reflect on what happened, or what's currently going on; what you did or are doing; and what you might have done or could be doing differently.

And here's a creative question that can provide a new perspective and generate fresh insights: *How would I advise someone else, someone like me, who is in a similar situation?* This one gives you a chance to step back, disentangle yourself from your emotional involvement, and take a more objective view.

PRACTICE

EXPANDING YOUR HORSE'S COMFORT ZONE

You may have come across the 'seven games' promoted in the Parelli natural horsemanship system. The first game is called the friendly game, and it's great for expanding the horse's comfort zone and improving the relationship between the two of you. While popularised by Pat and Linda Parelli, the friendly game has been around ever since horses and humans first got together. You'll need a halter, lead rope and a long lightweight stick – either a long twig from the hedge or a lungeing whip will do fine.

- ❖ 'Park' your horse so he is standing quietly on a loose rope, at a nice relaxed 3 or 4 on the spookability scale.

- ❖ Gently introduce the stick, keeping within his

comfort zone. He may be fine with you stroking him all over, scratching his back, and waving the stick around his head – or he may be worried about having it anywhere near him. Wherever the boundary of his comfort zone lies, that's fine. Notice any elevation on the spookability scale, and reduce your activities so he drops down to a 3 or 4 again.

❖ Keeping each session short and being careful not to over-stretch and frighten your horse, practise over a period of days, weeks and even months to gradually stretch your horse's comfort zone with regard to the stick. As the two of you progress, you can get more creative. For example, you could tie a plastic bag to the end of the stick, or a length of cloth, or – and please do this very, very carefully – something that rattles, like empty plastic bottles. Remember, the idea is to inspire your horse with confidence, not to terrify him!

Think of other ways to expand your horse's comfort zone and increase his tolerance for unusual and surprising incidents. For example, you could ask a friend to kick a large ball around, or roll tyres about, or push empty oil drums or barrels about, or whiz around on a bicycle, while you reassure the horse. Make sure you keep between him and the scary object, so that if he shies away from it, you don't get run over. If you remain steadfastly calm and reassuring, he'll learn that he can rely on your guidance under all circumstances. These exercises can be done with you leading the horse, and also, if you like, with you long-reining him. Long-reining has the advantage of accustoming him to accepting your leadership from behind him, which transfers easily across to your riding him.

CONFIDENCE-BOOSTING TIPS

There are several useful techniques to apply in a tight spot, and it's a good idea to practise them all beforehand so you'll be familiar with them and will remember to use them when you need them.

These methods are all good ways to bring out your natural qualities of calmness and courage while riding. It's not about trying to deceive yourself, but about genuinely changing how you feel. Applying these methods can help both you and your horse to stay at the low end of the spookability scale.

- ❖ Sit up straight. When humans are frightened, they curl up to protect the vulnerable front of the body. We all have this hedgehog tendency – it's biological. As you know, changing your physiology can change how you feel. Sitting up straight can help you to feel stronger and more determined.

- ❖ Singing is brilliant. I like chanting mantras, particularly that of the Buddha Tara. Her mantra is especially blessed to give us courage when we are afraid. It goes like this: *Om Ta-re Tu-ta-re Tu-re So-ha.* You can find various different tunes for it on YouTube. Or, if mantras aren't your thing, try this variation based on the chorus of an old song by Val Doonican: *Sit tall, ride high, look the whole world in the eye.* You'll find Val singing it on YouTube – it's actually called 'Walk Tall'.

- ❖ Breathing is always useful! When we're scared, our breathing tends to move high up in the chest, which is especially unhelpful for riders as it raises the centre of gravity, which weakens the seat. Practise breathing down into the hara area, and imagine breathing out down through your legs, to your feet, and then down into the ground.

❖ Talk encouragingly to yourself and your horse. Remember to say what you want, not what you don't want, so you phrase it positively, as in 'Let's be brave about this.' Praise both yourself and him frequently, as in 'Well done you!' for small triumphs such as taking some successful steps.

❖ Think of the many helpful coaching skills you've already acquired, such as creating a circle of confidence for you and your horse, or modelling another rider – or even modelling yourself as you are on those occasions when you're calm and courageous.

❖ Get into the habit of spotting the moments when you need to step in quickly to tell your horse what to do – don't leave it up to him to take over. Keep him busy so he stays focused on you.

❖ Shoulder-in is the marvellous, magical method for calming a horse. Practise it repeatedly until you can do it instantly, at any time. You don't have to do it dressage-test perfectly – it's effective just to pick up one rein and ask your horse to relax his jaw and flex to that side. If necessary, push him sideways with your inside leg, so you're in more of a leg-yield than a shoulder-in. This combines several elements: first, you're getting his attention and giving him something to do; second, you're relaxing his jaw; third, you're bending him; and fourth, you're moving him sideways, which alleviates the build-up of tension while making it difficult for him to take off. As all of this makes it easier for you manage him and harder for him to do anything silly, you'll feel more confident and he will feel safer and more inclined to trust your leadership and do what you tell him.

❖ If your horse is scared of a particular object, ask for shoulder-in or leg-yield with the horse facing towards the object. Many people say you should bend him away from it and ride on strongly, which is all very well if you can do it but doesn't suit everyone. By flexing the horse towards the object and encouraging him to sidle past, you are working with him rather than battling against him. This is a mark of good leadership, which will be appreciated by your horse.

❖ If necessary, get off the horse and lead him. By getting between him and the object you demonstrate to him that it's OK. Depending on the circumstances, you might be able to lead him past a few times, and then hop on again and ride him past. This may be less spectacular than having a heroic battle that sends you both rocketing up the spookability scale, but it's an elegant, low-key, non-confrontational approach that works very much better.

❖ Patience is a profound practice. If your horse won't go past something, stop trying to make him go. Just sit with him in a friendly way. Take all the pressure off, even the hope that he'll eventually move on (remember, he can pick up the slightest

mental pressure). Just sit quietly, enjoying the
present moment. Maybe the sun is shining;
perhaps there's a nice view; there might be some
delicious leaves in the hedge that you can pick and
offer to your horse. Relax, and soften, and
dissolve your own 'brace' at every level. This
includes letting go of your attachment to outcome:
in the great scheme of things, it really doesn't
matter whether or not your horse goes past this
object. When you have truly relaxed in loving
acceptance of whatever is happening, he will
probably go. But be careful – your acceptance
must be authentic, so that you are genuinely happy
whether he goes or whether he doesn't. And if
he doesn't go, and time's getting on and you need
to get home, then, with absolutely no
disappointment or resentment in your heart, you
can get off and lead him past, kindly, with love.
And you can be sincerely grateful to your horse
for teaching you the practice of patience and
ahimsa, or non-violence.

CHAPTER TWELVE:

COMPETITION COACHING

Performance coaching for competitive riding has become very popular, with techniques such as mental rehearsal, visualisation, goal-setting and anchoring for emotional states being recommended in the horse magazines and discussed on internet forums. Ideally, coaching should complement traditional instruction by addressing the parts that instruction doesn't usually reach, such as drawing out the 'deep structure' of modelling excellence and providing ways to clear psychological obstructions.

Do you want to compete?

Thinking about your aims, intentions and values can bring significant discoveries that could have a big impact on your success. Let's start with some gentle coaching questions.

Do you really want to compete? This is a deceptively simple question that can uncover a lot. Some riders don't really want to compete; they get roped into it because other people expect them to do it, or because they mistakenly think that riding is a sport and that must mean competing. Give these riders the idea that actually they don't have to do it – there are lots of other ways to enjoy being with their horses – and they are delighted to be let off the hook.

If, however, you've answered with an enthusiastic 'Yes!' let's ask another deceptively simple question: *Why?* What's important about it to you? Thinking about this will help to motivate you. Is it important for your own satisfaction? Do you want to prove something to yourself or to others? Do you enjoy the associated benefits of competing, for example the social aspects? Does the adrenalin buzz of an exciting, dangerous sport fire you up? Do you see this as a way to do justice to a fabulous, talented horse? Is competing important for you for professional reasons?

If your motives for competing are unclear, or are conflicting with other values, you'll lack the wholeheartedness and determination you need for success. Getting this out in the open will show you where the problem lies, so you can address it properly.

Conflicts of personal values can easily arise in the competitive sphere. There can be tremendous pressure to push your horse, both while competing and during training. Some activities are high risk for horses as well as for riders, such as steeplechasing and jumping cross-country fences. Harsh training practices are often employed to cut corners in dressage and show-jumping; there are even murky goings-on behind the scenes of the beauty contests of the showing world. Polo is particularly hard on horses; a horse dentist told me that he sees horrific cases of abused mouths in polo ponies. So it's good to see gentler forms of competition coming up now, such as Le Trec and horse agility, and also the use of video recording in dressage, which lets you do your test at home and avoid travelling long distances to competitions. Taking part in clinics and other instructional gatherings offers you another way to enjoy getting out and about socially with your horse, without the pressure of competing.

It's good to re-assess your motivation frequently, as your values naturally change over time. As a child I lived for show jumping, and was lucky in having a super pony who was good enough to win for both of us, but as I grew up my interests changed so that nowadays you couldn't drag me into a show ring with a tractor!

Does your horse want to compete?

Our next question concerns your horse. *Does he want to compete?* It's unlikely that even the most precocious foal says to his mum, 'I want to be a show jumper when I grow up.' Competition in the human sense is probably meaningless to a horse. However it's also true that some horses really do seem to like going to shows, enjoy taking part in the activities their riders sign them up for, and appreciate the praise and admiration when they do well.

It's important to find a suitable horse who is both willing and able to do whatever it is that you want to do. Trying to force a reluctant horse to compete is not only a miserable task for the rider, it's unkind to the horse and therefore morally dubious. Professional riders try out and discard many horses while searching for those that go on to be successful.

I sometimes come across a client who tells me that her horse performs beautifully at home, but seems to suffer from stage fright and fall apart in the ring when he goes to a show. If you have this problem, be very attentive to what's going on with you, the rider, when you're competing. It's a natural human tendency to tense up when nervous or excited. Sometimes the breathing will change, becoming high up in the chest – some people tell me they hardly breathe at all, they're so excited during a jumping round. A tense rider who isn't breathing is not going to bring out the best in a sensitive horse. The problem is not the horse's stage fright – it's the rider's tension. You can use the coaching skills you've already learned to help you manage your emotional state, plus the two exercises that follow in the Practice section will help you further.

Some horses get so over-excited at shows that they become unmanageable. Again, you already have lots of tips and techniques at your disposal. Allow yourself plenty of time to lead him about and then do some in-hand practice before asking him if he's ready to let you get on. And when you start riding him, the key lies in keeping him moving, keeping him busy and giving him interesting things to do in order to get him to focus on you. Again, the wonderful shoulder-in is indispensable. And here's a more radical idea: if your horse collects up and starts prancing when he's excited, why not encourage him to do a lovely natural piaffe? It's a great way of allowing him to express his excess energy in a way that is delightful for him and for you – and also for any spectators, who will be full of admiration!

PRACTICE

Coaching for competition riding includes pretty much everything we've already covered in this book. However there are two NLP exercises that are particularly useful for raising your game. The first exercise will help you to prepare for a competition, while the second one combines modelling, time-lining, anchoring and a circle of excellence to get you in the right state of mind for success.

PREPARING FOR SUCCESS

You remember the saying: 'To fail to prepare is to prepare to fail'? There's something rather tiresome about it: I imagine a prissy little person saying it, primly observing my characteristic chaos as I lose and forget essential items... This exercise is a good one for people like me! It's a more elaborate version of the one we did in Chapter Six, which was called Finding Solutions in the Future. It requires nothing more than a few minutes time, some imagination and creativity, and a pen and paper.

1 Identify the competition for which you want to prepare.

2 Imagine yourself at the competition, on the day, experiencing success. How would you know you're succeeding? Are you in the ring being given your rosette? Cantering round in a victory circuit holding your trophy? Are you flying joyfully over a jump? Performing a perfect extended trot? Galloping across the finish line? Identify a moment which for you perfectly captures your success at that event, and imagine enjoying that moment now, as vividly as you can.

3 From that vantage point in the future, imagine you could look back along a time-line that runs from that culminating point back to the present. Notice what the line looks like. From your vantage point in the future, reach out, take hold of the time-line, and give it a little shake. Shake it into alignment with your future success. Notice any changes to its appearance. What colour is it now?

4 From your future vantage point, look at the time-line which is now in alignment with your future success, and begin to identify the steps that have brought you to that success. Draw a line on your piece of paper, and write the steps alongside the line. Experiment with two lines, starting at the end point with one, and at the beginning point with the other; this second line will help you to fill in anything you might have overlooked on the first one.

5   Now return your attention fully to the present
moment, and look at what you've written. Add to
your notes as further steps occur to you in the
course of your preparing for success at the
competition.

6   And now remember to read your notes and follow
your own instructions as you prepare for the
competition!

THE MIND-STATE FOR SUCCESS

For this exercise you might find it helpful to refresh your memory of
the circle of excellence, in Chapter Four, and modelling, in Chapter
Seven. Like many NLP exercises, this one works especially well if you
follow the instructions to move about, although it also works well if
done armchair-style. If you're going to move about, allow yourself
plenty of room – maybe do it out in the field so you can run about and
entertain your horse at the same time. If you can find a friend to coach
you, that's ideal; if not, it's perfectly possible to coach yourself through
the exercise.

1   Identify the ideal mind-state that would help you
to succeed in your competition. For example, you
might need a combination of being calm, focused,
alert and sufficiently switched-on to be able to rise
to the occasion.

2   Standing at your present-moment place in the here
and now, imagine a future time-line going out in
front of you. Imagine it going far into the future,
all the way over the horizon, with the competition

day clearly marked on it in the near future. Leaving that future time-line in place, imagine a past time-line going out behind you, again all the way over the horizon. So now you are standing in the present moment with your future time-line in front of you and your past time-line behind you. What colour or colours are your future and past time-lines?

3   Cast your mind back over your past in search of previous occasions in which you experienced the ideal mind-state for success. It may have been at previous competitions or it may include other events in your life. Imagine yourself experiencing that mind-state now.

4   Begin moving slowly backwards along your past time-line, pausing at the places which resonate with your mind-state of success and allowing that mind-state to intensify at each place. There may or may not be memories of actual events associated with these places on your time-line.

5   When you've gone back far enough to have identified several instances of your mind-state of success, stop wherever you are on your past time-line and look ahead of you. In a moment, you're going to walk or even run forward along your time-line, scooping up all those instances of excellence in your hands and carrying them closely against your chest. You're going to run into your future, to the place on your future time-line that marks the competition day. Do that now – run along, scooping up your instances of excellence

and carrying them forward to the competition!

6   Whew! Stand at the place on your future time-line that marks the competition. Gather all those instances of excellence into your heart, and allow yourself to experience that mind-state of success as intensely as you can. If you could give it a colour, what colour would it be? Imagine yourself and your horse together being that colour, and also being surrounded by a circle of that colour, as though the two of you were in a spotlight of that colour.

7   Find a word that expresses this experience for you, and repeat this word several times as you imagine being in your spotlight, your circle of excellence, both you and your horse, experiencing that mind-state of success. Your word will anchor the experience, so you'll be able to recall the mind-state of success whenever you need it by repeating your anchor word. Identify something that will prompt you to use your word on the day – a sort of trigger for your anchor word. For example, seeing your horse's plaited mane in front of you could remind you: you see his mane, start reciting your word, and your mind-state of success arises strongly, just as you have practised. You might also use something to remind you of the colour of your circle of excellence – perhaps a tiny piece of coloured ribbon in your horse's mane, or on top of the headpiece of the bridle.

8   Leaving the experience of the mind-state of success on your future time-line, return to the

present moment on your time-line. Stand at the
present moment and relax. Look out at your
future time-line. Let the time-line be the same
colour as your circle of excellence. Remind
yourself of your anchor word. Imagine yourself
travelling along that time-line to the competition,
with the mind-state of success intensifying to
culminate in the competition. Imagine this several
times, so it becomes increasingly vivid for you.

9 Finish the exercise in any way that works for you.
Some people like to bring their time-lines into
their hearts; others prefer to dissolve them,
knowing they can re-create them at any time.

This is a powerful piece of coaching. Have a rest, and give yourself
some time to assimilate it.

CHAPTER THIRTEEN:
HORSE-FACILITATED COACHING FOR PERSONAL DEVELOPMENT

As riders and horse-people know, just being in the presence of a horse can be deeply therapeutic. Some years ago I went to a conference on 'Equine-facilitated learning' hosted by the British Horse Society. The BHS has long been a bastion of respectability in the horse world, and the fact that it was hosting the gathering might be taken to indicate that this sort of thing was becoming respectable. I remember almost no details about the meeting except for one outstanding sentence from the opening address, which was given by a senior staff member of the BHS. 'Our horses keep us sane,' she said.

The recognition of that simple truth underpins the wide range of horse-facilitated coaching and therapy that is now available. The high costs and logistical difficulties of employing horses as coaches and therapists place limits on accessibility to these services, but still the opportunities have greatly increased for more people to benefit from being with horses.

Perhaps the first clearly identified horse-facilitated therapy in the UK was Riding for the Disabled, which started in 1965. There are now over 800 local RDA groups in the UK. Other applications range from social programmes for disadvantaged children and young adults with difficulties, including drug and alcohol addiction, through business team-building and leadership trainings, to various kinds of coaching and therapy for private groups and individuals.

For the vast majority of people, who never come into contact with horses in their daily lives, it's easy to forget that humans and horses have had a deep affinity with each other for a very long time. Horses play a major part in human history; you could say that our civilisation rides on the back of the horse. But the connection is deeper than that. Horses are social creatures, and they're emotionally highly sensitive. They want to be friendly, and, fortunately for us, they're willing to be friends with us. They're willing to share with us not only their physical abilities of strength, speed and agility, but also their mental and emotional powers of sensitivity, communication, connection, joy and love.

Pegasus and Chiron

The mythical images of Pegasus, the flying horse, and Chiron, the centaur, half-horse and half-human, are deeply meaningful. In shamanic and mythological thought, the horse can fly between the different realms of existence and is willing and able to take a human to these other realms. Pegasus can carry us to the different realms or domains of the mind that can be hard to find unaided. And in Greek mythology the centaur Chiron is famed for his ability to heal, or make whole. By connecting with a horse one becomes more than an ordinary human, and the horse becomes more than an ordinary horse; together we become a marvellous centaur.

Connecting deeply with a horse can awaken our awareness of our connection with the universe; it can heal the existential sense of alienation so many humans experience, and bridge the rift between 'humanity' and 'nature'. While this is deeply fulfilling for the individuals concerned, it also has a wider significance. Human pride, self-centredness and chauvinism are terribly damaging, blocking both our outer connection with our fellow beings and our inner connection with our own true nature. Many people working in the fields of eco-psychology and deep ecology believe that these two disconnections are at the bottom of our exploiting our fellow humans and other beings and trashing the planet that is home for us all. (Joanna Macy's excellent workshops and writings offer a good example; her 'Work that Reconnects' directly addresses these two disconnections.)

A typical session

There is a wide diversity of approaches in horse-facilitated coaching and therapy, so what follows is just one example out of many options. This particular presentation refers to the kind of one-to-one coaching that I typically offer clients who want to work with my horses.

Although it isn't essential to work on a specific issue, doing so can help to focus the session. This may seem extraordinary, but you can project an aspect of your issue onto a horse, and, if the horse agrees to work with you, he or she will behave accordingly. So, for example, if you want to explore a relationship problem, the horse can play the role of your partner or child or colleague or whoever. Or, if your issue is not about a personal relationship, the horse can play the role of an inanimate object. (I once asked a big black mare to represent a filing cabinet, which she did perfectly!) I know this sounds weird but it is true.

We begin the session with a bare minimum of theory, starting with the psychology of horses and how their flight responses are so helpful to humans, and going on to talk about how we as humans experience being in the world.

The descriptive model of the poached egg works well for most people. This depicts our experience of being in the world in terms of two concentric circles; the outer one is the circle of conditioning, the inner one the circle of authenticity. The outer circle of conditioning includes our fears and pretences, beliefs and identities, memories, hopes and fantasies; our stories about ourselves and the world; our adopting of other people's criticisms and expectations of us; our strategies and techniques, habits and limited past-based reactions. It's the realm of separation, comparison, attachment, aversion, fear, confusion, duality and concepts of self and other. The inner circle of authenticity, which is often hidden by the outer circle, is the realm of openness, space and spontaneity, present-moment pure response; genuine creativity; connection; love and joy. Horses can help us to find that authentic realm and meet them in that space – a glimpse of a different level of being and a wonderful experience for both human and horse.

For most people the practical part of the session usually falls into two or three phases.

First, we find a way for you to venture beyond your normal comfort zone with a task for you to do with the horse that will stretch you. This allows you to explore various things that come up when you're stretched, such as success criteria, beliefs, default habitual programmes, and the various strategies of the circle of conditioning. My job here is to encourage you to notice and assess what's going on with yourself, with the horse, and with the interaction between the two of you. This first task may range from simply approaching the horse, which is a challenge in itself for someone who is nervous of horses, to something that will stretch someone who is experienced with horses and has lots of expert techniques at their fingertips.

Next, we bring in some more active coaching. You have an opportunity to experiment with 'doing things differently'. The horse will give you immediate feedback as to how he is experiencing your presence and your behaviour and this will enable you to monitor your own process. You may find some new, more effective strategies – or you may find yourself moving to a different level of being altogether that is beyond strategy and technique: the circle of authenticity. This is where any spectators who are experienced horse-people might gasp with amazement as they see somebody make a connection of such purity with the horse that the horse responds by doing something extraordinary. However your shift manifests, we make sure that you really get the physical experience of it and we anchor it by word, posture and gesture so you'll be able to find it again.

Lastly, step three is about establishing the learning and being able to apply it amid uncertainty. We may work with the horse at liberty; after all, you'll want to take your learning home with you and the other people in your life are not on the ends of ropes! We'll also do some future pacing which will help you to apply what you've learned when you need it later.

Inner and outer aspects

There are some common elements that emerge in many therapeutic encounters with humans and horses. And, as with any interaction, there are outer and inner aspects.

Outwardly, an observer would see a human student learning how to handle a horse effectively on the ground: haltering, leading, moving around, and being with the horse in such a way that both human and horse are evidently enjoying each other's company.

Inwardly, the student is learning how to find inside herself the qualities that allow for such an effective interaction, such as positive intention, awareness, mindfulness, trustworthiness, empathy, warmth, humour, creativity, patience, confidence, respect, emotional stability and authenticity. She has the opportunity to drop her story, all the conceptual stuff that goes to construct a personal ego-level identity, which doesn't interest the horse, and to experience a deeper level of being. She has a chance to experience shifts within herself, with the horse's responses providing undeniable evidence of those shifts, and she can glimpse the possibilities of making lasting changes in herself and in her life.

I find that my horses love taking part in coaching sessions, actively coming forward to meet people and usually deciding between themselves who is going to take on a particular student. The key point is that the benefits of a therapeutic encounter are necessarily reciprocal. There must be no hint of exploitation, of one person using another or benefiting at another's expense. It's only when the human stops seeing the horse as 'other' and starts connecting with a deeper, shared level of being that the real magic happens. And horses love to be with humans who are willing to meet them in the open space of mutual understanding and connection.

In a way there's no need to make too much of it. It happens naturally to some degree in any friendly horse-human interaction. The coaching process just makes the process easier and more obvious and encourages the student to acknowledge the significance of what's happening.

After all this rather theoretical, heady stuff, I hope the following accounts of real coaching sessions with Brigit and Rowan will bring it more to life.

Real-life accounts

Jenny came to us on the recommendation of her psychotherapist, who accompanied her on her visit. Jenny was experiencing a lot of fear and anxiety, had extremely low self-esteem, and was prone to bouts of weeping. When she met Brigit and Rowan, she was drawn to Rowan. Rowan is naturally sweet and gentle, also very bright with a mischievous sparkle. Jenny took a while to find the courage to approach him, although he was secured to a fence and standing quietly. Gradually she was able to move closer to him, and as she relaxed enough to be open to his friendliness, she asked if she might groom him. She spent most of the session brushing and talking with Rowan. She also talked with her therapist, although several times she asked her therapist to step back so she could just be alone with Rowan. During the session Rowan was apparently processing Jenny's intense emotions (horses have the ability to do this for humans: they seem to be able to allow the emotions to pass through their bodies and dissipate), and Jenny was becoming calmer and happier and more able to simply enjoy being in his presence; she also greatly enjoyed his evident appreciation of her caring for him.

Subsequently, Jenny's therapist reported that Jenny found that the session gave her the opportunity to experience simply allowing her emotions to flow through her, without becoming distressed by them; this was a revelation for her. She also found Rowan's steady acceptance and appreciation of her deeply reassuring – he provided a model for her to relate to herself more steadfastly and kindly; and she was able to relax and simply enjoy herself in his company – again, an unusual experience for her.

Sally wanted to work on a particular issue: following an extended period of intense domestic difficulties, she was aware of having protected herself from the trauma by distancing herself from her family; now she wanted to explore reconnecting emotionally. As she was an experienced horse-person we started with both horses at once, both at liberty. At the start of the session, the horses ignored Sally: they went over to the furthest corner of the arena to chat with some other horses who were the other side of the fence. Sally and I sat down and talked for a few minutes; then ran through a simple NLP exercise that enabled her to make an emotional shift. As she made the shift, both horses swung round and looked straight at her, then together they walked over and nuzzled her, resting their heads in her lap as she stroked them.

The horses recognised the emotional shift Sally had made and provided her with their external corroboration of her inner experience; their loving response and physical contact also enabled her to go more deeply into the shared experience of the emotional connection she was seeking.

Susan was experiencing general bodily stiffness and shooting pains in her legs, especially the knees. She had been the primary support for a family member for a long time, and she was exhausted. She was aware of feeling unsupported herself, and in desperate need of some kind of nurturing. As we sat in the barn with the horses, who were munching on haynets as we talked, the image of a rearing horse came up for Susan. The horse was fixed in a rearing 'levade' posture, like a warhorse, but although it looked noble and strong its hind legs were trembling with exhaustion. When I asked Susan what prevented the horse from descending from the levade, a cobra emerged, hood extended, looking fierce. At first Susan found this a frightening image, but when I remarked that the naga, appearing as cobra with extended hood, is a Buddhist icon often portrayed as protecting the meditating Buddha, she realised that it might represent a protector part of herself. We asked the cobra to allow the rearing horse to lower its forefeet to the ground, and it agreed. As the horse lowered its feet, Susan found herself relaxing and breathing deeply.

At this point Rowan looked up from his haynet, walked over to where we were sitting, and lay down next to Susan. Susan then lay down next to him. A few moments later, Rowan stretched himself flat on the ground and placed one foreleg over Susan's body, holding her close. They lay like that for maybe five minutes before Rowan moved, and they both got up.

On getting up, Susan noticed that the pains in her legs had diminished and she felt relaxed and peaceful and full of love. Before ending the session we discussed how she might find different ways of supporting the family member and of getting the support she herself needed.

Gill was attending a workshop with several other people. She revealed on arrival that she was frightened of horses and that one of her main aims for the day was to work with this fear.

We allocated some time at the beginning of the workshop for each person to meet Brigit and Rowan individually, and, although normally the horses would not be wearing halters or be in any way restricted for this particular type of workshop, on this occasion I put halters on them to reassure Gill.

We all went into the field, and the humans sat on the ground in a circle; Gill and two others chose to sit in chairs. The horses were wandering around, joining the circle for the activities that interested them. Both horses were gently attentive to Gill throughout the morning, and she was visibly relaxing in their presence. I removed their halters towards the end of the morning session.

After the lunch break, Gill chose to sit on the ground for the afternoon session. Brigit and Rowan walked up together to stand on either side of her, just behind her, as though guarding her. Gill spontaneously lay back and stretched out her arms; the horses stepped closer until they were standing over her outspread arms as she lay flat on her back on the grass. A stillness and silence arose among all of us, and we all stayed as though spellbound for several minutes. Then both horses moved slowly away from Gill, backing carefully over her arms, and began grazing peacefully nearby. When Gill sat up, tears were running down her smiling face – we were all moved and a bit tearful.

Gill reported later that this encounter had a profound effect on her, enabling her to release some 'gloopy nonsense' that had been holding her back, and freeing her up to realise her strengths and her sense of purpose.

PRACTICE

There's a bit of background we need to go into before we go into the practical exercise, which is called a Mandala practice.

Many people are familiar with the Sanskrit word 'mandala'. It can have a wide range of meanings. Probably the one that comes to mind for most people is the mandala that is pictorially represented by a circle, often with a central figure and sometimes with other figures around the periphery. This represents how we experience our world, as a figure in the centre of our surroundings. If you were in a flat place, like a flat plain, your horizon would be all around you in a circle. So your personal mandala consists of yourself at the centre of a surrounding space which is bounded by a circular perimeter. You really are the centre of your world!

How we occupy that centre, the quality of being that we bring to it, affects both how we perceive our mandala and also how effective we are within it. There are practices which can help us to occupy our centre in such a way as to be at ease and empowered in our world – not as some kind of nutty ego-trip, but in a healthy way.

Practising with a horse either in a round pen or lungeing can be a wonderful way to learn how to occupy the centre of our mandala effectively. Here is an example of a client, Vanessa, practising with the help of Brigit.

Vanessa has come to see us because she feels depleted and exhausted. Tearfully, she explains that she has just come out of an emotionally draining relationship and is having difficulty focusing on anything; she feels that her energy is scattered, as though she were not fully present. She has had limited experience with horses; she likes them, and is happy to be with Brigit, but has no technical knowledge of how to lunge a horse. Brigit and I demonstrate a couple of times; Vanessa is absolutely right – she is having trouble focusing! At last she sort of gets the idea, and feels ready to have a go. Vanessa droops miserably in the middle while Brigit plods round her in a potato-shaped circuit, pulling towards the gate and cutting in on the other side of the circle. After several such uninspired circuits, Brigit starts to cut in too close for comfort and Vanessa is obliged to wake up, pull herself together and raise her energy in order to stay safe. Taking more interest now in what's going on, she begins to experiment with connecting with Brigit with more mental and emotional engagement. She begins to stand up straighter, with a stronger posture. Suddenly there is a big shift: it's as though Vanessa kind of switches on, and Brigit is instantly transformed from a plodding horse to a beautiful Arab mare, walking with grace and sureness. Vanessa is standing strong at the centre of her mandala, smiling, fully present, with Brigit walking gracefully around the perimeter in a perfect circle, no longer pulling out or cutting in. Together they look radiant as they manifest the mandala of completion, wholeness and perfection.

So now you can guess where we're going with this practice session – you're going to ask your horse to help you to manifest your own mandala of perfection!

You'll need a halter, a lunge line and a lunge whip or long stick, and a quiet place in which to practise.

❖ Start by connecting with your horse in a friendly way, and explain what you would like to do. Now, here comes the really interesting bit for expert horse people. You're going to abandon your expert horsy techniques, because this exercise is not about techniques. It's about you!

❖ Stand in the centre of the circle, the centre of your mandala, and invite your horse to walk around you in a circle.

❖ Notice what's going on with you. How do you feel? What thoughts are coming up? What impulses? Where is your energy? How are you standing?

❖ Now for some multi-tasking. As you experiment with making changes, you need to notice how your horse responds. So your focus needs to expand to include both the centre of your mandala – yourself – and the perimeter of your mandala – your horse. Here are some ideas for you to experiment with:

- expand your awareness to reach out to your horse;
- withdraw your awareness to exclude your horse;
- raise your energy higher in your body, then lower it again;
- breathe differently – high and fast, then slower, down into the hara;
- imagine your feet have roots going down into the ground;
- imagine that your body is made of light, and so is your horse's – you're both beautiful, radiant beings with bodies made of light;
- remember a time when you felt completely happy, and allow yourself to feel like that now;
- trust your natural creativity to come up with your own ideas for experiments to try.

❖ However your horse responds, respect his feedback – and change yourself to inspire him differently.

When you've done enough, thank your horse for his help, and reflect on what you've learned. How might you apply your learnings, both with your horse and elsewhere in your life?

CHAPTER FOURTEEN:

HOW TO WORK WITH A RIDING

INSTRUCTOR

I find that many of the riders who come to me with confidence issues don't actually have a problem with lack of confidence; they have a problem with lack of riding skill. They're scared because they feel unsafe, and that's because they really are unsafe – their limited riding abilities are putting them at risk. In these cases the solution lies not in confidence coaching, but in riding lessons.

Whatever sort of riding you do, it's true to say that the better you ride, the more you and your horse will enjoy yourselves. While you can learn a lot from books and the internet, nothing beats real-life hands-on personal instruction. So in this chapter we're going to look at how you can apply your coaching skills to help you to get more out of your riding lessons.

The ideal instructor

It's a rare person who has the multi-skills of understanding and getting along with both horses and humans, riding well herself, and being able to teach others. If you've found an instructor like this, thank your lucky stars and hold on tight to her!

Let's have a more detailed look at some of the attributes such a teacher would have.

❖ She would be kind, encouraging and easy to talk to, with a good sense of humour. Humour is often overlooked as an important quality for effective teaching. I train with Perry Wood, who has a great sense of humour which he uses to good effect when giving a lesson. Once, when helping me to improve my 'feel', he told me to close my eyes and put my attention into my seat. I was riding Rowan, who in those days was living up to his nickname of the Ginger Fizz, so I explained that I was scared to close my eyes in case he took off. Whereupon Perry reassured me: 'That's OK – you close your eyes, and I'll tell you if he takes off so you can open them again!' Which was so ridiculous that I had to laugh, which relaxed me. I closed my eyes, Rowan stayed underneath me, and sure enough my sense of feel improved!

❖ She would be willing to listen to you and also to your horse. Many instructors teach lessons according to their own agenda, without asking you what you want to learn. Even if you tell them, they don't listen. And if your horse says, 'Look, I'm really struggling with this,' they don't listen to him either.

❖ She would be emotionally stable, patient, and not prone to strops. I remember an instructor from my childhood who would get angry if her students made a mistake. When one of my friends fell off during a lesson one day, this horrible woman stood over the poor child – who was winded and gasping for breath like a goldfish – and said, icily: 'I really don't see how I can be expected to teach you when you're sitting on the floor. Get back on that pony and this time stay on it!'

❖ She would be knowledgeable, experienced and competent, and willing to admit when she doesn't know something, or if she has misjudged the ability of the horse or rider. I was impressed by the Portuguese trainer Rodrigo Matos when he was teaching a clinic here on Exmoor a few years ago. He was instructing a rider in the piaffe. He tried one way; it didn't work. He tried another way; that didn't work either. He tried a third way; still no good. So he simply said, 'OK, we stop this now. I have asked too much.' At no time did he blame either the rider or the horse; he had several different approaches to offer, and when none worked he took responsibility for having over-estimated their abilities – his fault, not theirs.

❖ She would be able to communicate her instructions clearly, so you can understand them. It takes a special skill for someone who is a good rider to be able to identify exactly how she does something, so she can tell you how to do it too. And she needs to be aware of more than just the techniques; she needs to understand the 'deep structure' as well.

❖ She would be careful with regard to the safety of
you and your horse. This sounds obvious but,
even in these days of heightened awareness of
'health and safety', it's astonishing how casual some
instructors are about the safety of their students.
I have come across some hair-raising incidents,
one of the worst cases being the Pony Club
instructor who gave a jumping lesson in which she
made the children jump with their ponies strapped
up in side reins to prevent them putting their
heads down to eat grass!

❖ She would be willing and able to demonstrate
when necessary, which might include riding your
horse. If the instructor is afraid to get on your
horse because she doesn't think he is safe to ride,
then she really shouldn't be encouraging you to
get on him. If the horse is not a 'safe conveyance'
(a marvellous term – not mine – I've borrowed it
from a client who had a bucking mare who was
described by the physio as 'unlikely ever to be a
safe conveyance'), then the necessary steps must
be taken to prepare him to become one before
anyone gets on.

How to help your instructor to coach you more effectively

Taking lessons from a riding instructor introduces some interesting and
sometimes conflicting dynamics. On the one hand, she is the expert in
a position of relative authority, which can make you feel rather junior
and disempowered. On the other hand, you are employing her, so
you're actually the boss, and it's absolutely vital that you take
responsibility for what is happening and are clear as to what is and is

not OK with you. Most importantly, you owe it to yourself and your horse to never let an instructor persuade you into doing anything you'll regret, such as causing your horse distress.

It helps your instructor if you set aside a few minutes at the start of your lesson to chat about what you want, both overall aims regarding your particular interests, strengths and areas for improvement, and also specific aims for the individual lesson. A good instructor will also help you to clarify your goals and explore options.

It helps your instructor, during the lesson, if you tell her when either you or your horse needs a break. Also, for heaven's sake tell her immediately if you can't hear her clearly, if you don't understand an instruction, or if for any reason you can't comply with an instruction.

It also helps your instructor if you stop a few minutes before the end of the lesson so you have time to go over what you've learned and how you can move forward with it. Make sure you've understood everything correctly, and ask her to set you homework.

Although we hope you'll find your lessons helpful and enjoyable, so you can wholeheartedly say, 'Thanks – that was super!', there are bound to be occasions when things don't go so well. You may need to find ways to give feedback to your instructor about her teaching, and even to disagree with her, without causing offence. You may remember the 'feedback sandwich' from Chapter Seven: tell the person about something you liked, then mention what you'd like to be different, then tell her about something else you liked. Phrase the sandwich filling positively, and take responsibility for your part in what happened; for example: 'I wonder if next lesson we could spend even more time explaining each exercise; I felt we rather rushed through it and I got a bit lost. Actually, I need to go slower generally – I need more breaks to rest and to assimilate all the new information.' Saying it like this is unlikely to upset her and set her thinking she's a rubbish teacher. And if you need to disagree about something, you can do that equally constructively; for example: 'You know, I'm really unhappy about the idea of putting him in a stronger bit; I'd like to find another way of doing it. I'm happy to put the work in to improve my riding and give him more schooling, and I'd love it if you'd help us with that.'

It's important to remember that a good teacher should encourage you, not intimidate you. If you're too frightened to talk to her, maybe you need to find a more approachable instructor.

Alexander Technique instructors

Many riding instructors – and many riders – concentrate their efforts on improving the horse. It can be a revelation to take a different approach, such as having a lesson from a riding teacher who is trained in the Alexander Technique. Such a teacher concentrates on you – your position, balance and breathing. You're going along, almost ignoring the horse – and then suddenly, as though miraculously, you notice that he is moving differently – more freely, better balanced, and much, much more happily!

I remember watching one particularly striking Alexander Technique demonstration. Two women had bravely volunteered to be the guinea pigs; they came into the arena on big dressage-type horses and rode round looking stiff and inelegant, with a lot of pushing and pulling going on. When the teacher stopped them and asked each rider about herself and her riding, each woman replied with a long list of her horse's faults – while saying nothing at all about herself. The teacher asked them to get off their horses and to sit in chairs. One at a time, she adjusted each woman's posture in the chair. Then she put the first rider back on the horse and began to adjust her posture in the saddle, shortening the stirrups a couple of holes. As the horse walked around, the teacher kept making tiny adjustments to his rider. The horse began to walk more freely. The worry lines on his face smoothed out and he started to smile. With the rider so focused on her own position that she was oblivious to the horse, the audience started to applaud with delight as the horse walked increasingly beautifully, the rider sitting in perfect balance with his movement. There was no more pushing and pulling. It was like magic! Then the teacher did the same thing with the other rider. More magic – and another happy, smiling horse, able to move freely to express his natural beauty.

Co-coaching with friends

Lastly, don't underestimate the power of a little help from your friends. Co-coaching can be great fun and very useful. Even people who don't ride at all can help by reminding you of things you need to remember. You can give them a list of pointers to call out, such as prompts to breathe down into the hara, or to bring your attention to your seat, or to relax and enjoy yourself. And if you can find a helper with a good store of jokes, well, then you're really laughing!

CHAPTER FIFTEEN:

KEEPING YOUR HORSE AT LIVERY

It might seem a bit odd to include a chapter on keeping a horse at livery in a book on how to be your own coach. However, difficulties with livery yards rank high on many horse-owners' lists of problems, and it may be helpful to consider how coaching principles could be helpful in dealing with them.

We've already mentioned the importance of environment for your horse's happiness, and how difficulties with his home life can cause problems for you when you're trying to ride him. Some of the issues are more to do with tricky logistics, while others are more to do with tricky humans, whether those running the yard or fellow clients.

Logistics

Let's look first at some of the common logistical problems, many of which are to do with the complications of your horse's social life.

Your horse needs company, but keeping him in the same field as others can be hazardous. I know of several deaths from broken legs due to kicking. The risks are greater if any of the horses are shod; if they are in a mixed group of mares and geldings; if there are too many horses in the space available; if there is not enough food for them; if they are given hay or bucket feeds in the field; if the herd is subjected to the insecurity of horses coming and going; and if a bully horse upsets the dynamics of an otherwise friendly herd.

Many people decide the risks are too great, so they separate the horses into individual paddocks, often fenced with electric tape. This can mean lonely isolation in tiny enclosures, often without adequate shelter from the weather or from flies.

Another logistical issue associated with horses' social lives is that of people moving horses and leaving behind one animal who goes nuts at being left. There's a lot written about 'separation anxiety' nowadays in the horse magazines and on the internet, often discussing it as though it were some kind of neurosis or pathological disorder. But separation anxiety is normal for horses. They are social animals, and they naturally find it extremely stressful to be abandoned by the rest of the herd. The abandoned horse may injure himself careering around, or he may jump out of the field or break out of his stable. He may work himself up into such a state that you can't do anything with him when you arrive, hoping to ride.

The logistics of feeding can also be difficult for owners. It's not always possible to get to the yard first thing in the morning and last thing at night to ensure that your horse is not left for long periods without food. Your horse needs to eat more or less continuously, but if you have to shut him in overnight from 4pm to 10am it's difficult to provide enough hay to keep him stocked up for 18 hours. This means he endures long periods with an empty tummy, becoming increasingly anxious and, quite possibly, developing stomach ulcers as he sees and hears his neighbours being fed while he goes hungry.

Humans

All these issues can be tackled with the support and co-operation of helpful, understanding people at the yard. So no problems there then...!

In the previous chapter I mentioned the BHS lady's remark, 'Our horses keep us sane.' Given that so many horse people seem to be really rather nutty, one wonders how much nuttier they would be if they didn't have horses? Even if they are OK with the horses, they are often, um, challenged when it comes to dealing with humans.

Some livery yard owners don't seem to realise that they are running a business, and that rule number one of running a business is 'Keep the customers happy'. The owners of one yard I was at had apparently re-written this rule to read 'Make the customers cry'! They reduced nearly every client to tears, whether of misery, frustration or fury, and bullied one woman so badly that she was sobbing into her horse's mane almost every day. People in the horse world are sometimes behind the times; some haven't yet caught up with the fact that riding schools and livery yards are now part of the leisure industry and running a livery yard is rather like running a hotel – and while the Fawlty Towers approach is hilarious on TV it's not so funny in real life.

There's also the issue of client compatibility. Even if the owners are fine, and the other clients are OK, you'll enjoy yourself much more if you're with compatible people. If you like hacking and hanging out with your horse, you may not fit in with a yard full of very competitive riders.

Keeping horses with like-minded friends is wonderful, providing company, help, shared facilities (and therefore reduced costs), and much more fun for you and your horse. A good set-up will make such a huge difference to your enjoyment and to your horse's happiness that it may be worth paying a bit extra, or travelling a bit further to get to the right place.

Coaching tips to deal with difficulties

How ever careful you are to find the right place, difficulties can still arise simply due to the inevitable frictions of a bunch of humans getting together. Let's look now at some coaching tips for how to deal with the most common problems found in livery yards: communication difficulties and bullying.

Negotiation

Skilful negotiation allows everyone involved to feel that their needs have been respected.

We all know what it's like to have our needs ignored when somebody manipulates or bullies us into going along with what they want. It leaves us feeling resentful and angry with the other person. So it's easy to appreciate the sense in learning to negotiate skilfully.

There's a magic question that can help you to negotiate with other people. It's a variation of a question we've already seen in previous chapters: *'What needs to be different, for this to work for you?'* (The 'this' refers to whatever it is that you want to happen and the other person is unhappy about.)

Ask the question genuinely, with a sincere willingness to understand and respect the other person's needs, and allow time for her to answer. It could be one thing that needs to change, or it could be several. Or it could be that whatever you want is just not going to be acceptable to the other person – in which case you need to rethink your plans, taking her needs into account.

How interesting!

Humans are weird. They do incomprehensible things. Sometimes this is OK: we just mentally put it in the 'weirdity' basket and forget it. But sometimes it's not OK: somebody does something so hurtful or destructive that we can't just forget it, and the more we think about it the more upset we become.

Next time somebody does something weird, instead of reacting with anger or incredulity or impatience, try responding in your own mind like this: *'How interesting!'* Then follow up that initial 'How interesting!' with some questions to reflect on, to explore why the person might have behaved like this. What might they believe, that they would do this? What might be important to them? What might they want to achieve? What might have happened in their past, that has contributed to their behaving like this?

Your immediate response of 'How interesting!' can turn your thoughts in this more constructive direction, so you can gain some understanding of where the other person might be coming from. Then, if necessary, you'll be better placed to take appropriate action.

How to say 'No' nicely

People are often afraid to say 'No'. We may be afraid of offending the other person or hurting their feelings, or we may think they'll be angry with us. The problem is that if we're too scared to say 'No' we'll find ourselves getting railroaded into doing things that we'll regret.

We need to be able to set boundaries, and this requires our being able to say 'No'. More than that, we need to be able to say 'No' nicely – which means communicating clearly while also being considerate of the other person's feelings.

Think of a situation in which you'd like to say 'No', and you're worried about how the other person might react. Now, in your mind, experiment with different ways of saying 'No', imagining the other person's possible responses to each different way you say it. Although you're not responsible for their response, how you say 'No' is likely to influence them, so you'll want to say it in a way that is likely to lead to a favourable response.

If possible, practise in front of a mirror, so you can see yourself saying 'No' in various ways. Be creative. Try snarling ferociously. Try speaking gently. Experiment until you come up with a whole-hearted 'No' that satisfies you as being both clear and kind.

Bullying

Sadly, a lot of people experience bullying at livery yards, often from other clients. People bully others for various reasons. Maybe they have grown up in a family where aggressive behaviour is accepted as normal, and they think it's OK to behave like that. Maybe they are mentally and emotionally immature or have psychological problems; a mentally and emotionally healthy person doesn't want to bully others.

Bullying is about power and control. Bullies try to boost themselves by exerting power over others. They often target someone they see as being 'different' in some way, such as having a different physical appearance, or accent, or family background. If there is nothing obvious, a bully may make something up as an excuse to justify their behaviour. Whatever form the bullying takes, there is no excuse for it; any so-called 'reason' for it is irrelevant. Bullying is about the bully, not about the bully's target.

You can prepare yourself to deal with bullying by mentally rehearsing your response. A good way to respond to verbal aggression is to ignore *what* the person is saying, and focus instead on *how* they are saying it. So instead of being distracted by their words, you answer their emotion.

For example you could say, calmly and politely: 'I'm sorry you're upset. But there's no need for you to be so aggressive.'

This answer acknowledges the other person's feelings while drawing attention to their aggressive behaviour, without getting distracted by what they're saying about you. You're shifting the focus onto the bully and away from yourself. You're also inviting them to look at their behaviour and their feelings – and maybe, just maybe, there's a chance that they might think about what they're doing.

Sometimes other people might try to interfere with what you're doing with your horse, not because they're bullying you, but because they genuinely want to be helpful. The problem is that they are suggesting things that really are not helpful! For example, Chris had no end of 'help' offered with Martin. People advised her to hit Martin to make him go – 'He's just being naughty and you have to show him who's boss.' They also criticised her for not riding him – 'For heaven's sake, either get on and ride the horse or get rid of it.' None of this was intended to be hurtful, but Chris found it utterly demoralising. In such cases it can be hard to think clearly and find the courage to stand up for what you believe in. It can be a huge relief to find someone who can support you, whether a friend or a coach or an instructor; even a book that endorses your values and helps you find ways to explain your approach can be a great support.

Friends

The better you are at communicating and negotiating and generally getting along with the other people at your yard, the better for all of you. There are always logistical problems in keeping horses, especially if you live some distance away and have other things to attend to, such as work and family. These problems are so much more easily managed with the help of others. In addition, the friends you make through a shared love of horses will be among the best of friends – second only to the horses themselves. I once kept Brigit at a very happy yard when I was living in a rented house with no facilities to keep her at home. The owners and the other clients were all friendly and helpful. We arranged to share the chores during the week, and then we all got together at the weekends, often hanging out with each other and our horses for the whole day. So a good yard can work well – and it's worth persevering to find one that works well for you.

APPENDIX:
BITLESS AND BAREFOOT

There's a rapidly growing movement among horse people towards managing horses in ways that are intended to be both kinder and more natural.

I'm very drawn to these ideals myself, and in the Further Reading section at the end of this book I've included some relevant books and websites that I particularly like. In this Appendix I want to discuss some points that I hope you'll find interesting and useful in helping you to find your way around the range of various schools of thought emerging with regard to horsemanship.

Background

Most conventional horsemanship is based on the assumption that humans are superior to other animals, perhaps not always physically but certainly intellectually, morally, spiritually and ontologically. This assumption of superiority leads to a second assumption: that human needs and wishes are more important than those of other beings. These two assumptions, which go back a very long way and are deeply embedded in our culture, have been justified by religious ideas, particularly those of the three theistic religions of Judaism, Christianity and Islam, and also by scientific ideas, particularly schemes of evolution which place humans at the top of the tree.

On the basis of these assumptions of superiority and priority humans have long exploited animals, such exploitation being generally accepted as normal and even right and proper. Questioning the assumptions and challenging the morality of such exploitation is extremely subversive and potentially colossally disruptive to human society. Much farming and food production and scientific and medical research, as well as many leisure activities and sports, and even keeping pets, could become unacceptable if we dared to challenge beliefs in the God-given or scientifically sanctioned right to exploit animals for human purposes.

However, increasing numbers of people are now making these subversive challenges. The ease of communication provided by the internet is helping to spread the message. There are links with the environmental movement, which is gaining urgency and intensity in the face of increasing global crises, and which, at its radical core of deep ecology, is asking profound questions concerning the nature of being and of the interdependence of all life. If you thought the new ideas in the horse world were limited to a handful of eccentrics who like riding bareback – think again! They are part of a much larger movement that could turn human civilization upside down.

So, energised and perhaps inspired by this background context, let's take a look at some of the new ideas in horsemanship that are emerging.

Not riding

In addition to quite widespread doubts being raised as to the ethics of using horses for obviously hazardous and often cruel sports such as polo, rodeo-riding and steeplechasing, there's a much smaller but very serious dialogue taking place about the ethics of riding horses at all. While I think it's wonderful that these questions are being raised, and I can see that quite a lot of riding is more or less miserable for horses, I can't agree with those who think that all riding is necessarily wrong. It seems evident to me that many horses greatly enjoy carrying a friendly human; more than that, there is a deeply fulfilling mutual delight to be found in the centaur experience, shared by a horse and a human, which is most easily found when riding and which some horses will actively seek out. Meanwhile, for those people who want to continue riding and competing but are concerned about the ethics of doing so, gentle riding sports such as Le Trec are gaining popularity, as are equestrian activities that don't involve riding, such as horse agility.

Not rugging or stabling

Some people wishing to promote more natural lifestyles for their horses are leaving their animals out in fields all the time, without rugs. I'm concerned about this trend. It's fine to leave a native pony out unrugged, as long as there is adequate shelter from the wind and rain in the winter and from biting insects in the summer, but how could anyone think it's OK to leave an unprotected horse out in the open, up to its hocks in mud in the winter and being eaten alive by flies in the summer? Modern riding horses, with Arabian ancestors from hot dry countries, are not suited to cold wet climates; they get mud fever and rain scald, and they suffer horribly. If you don't want to stable your horses, then a field with a warm dry shed with clean bedding is a good solution. The shed must have two doors; if it has only one door the horses won't go inside for fear of being trapped in it.

Not shoeing

Keeping horses unshod is becoming quite common. Both my horses, lightweight Arabs with tough feet, are barefoot. It works for some horses but not for all, and a fundamentalist rigidity on the part of a human can cause suffering for the poor horse who is obliged to hobble about on sore feet to satisfy the owner's determination to be 'natural'. Suitability for bare feet isn't entirely predictable: I know of a young Andalusian, who had never been shod, who was unable to go barefoot when ridden and had to have shoes; conversely a hefty middle-aged cob who had been shod all her life was fine from the start when her owner decided to try her barefoot. It's important to be careful about diet and to keep the weight down: it's thought that many horses are 'footy' due to low-grade inflammation of the laminae. It seems that shoes, in addition to protecting the wall of the hoof, have a kind of numbing effect on the foot which masks slight lameness; when you take the shoes off the soreness becomes apparent. Some riders whose horses can't manage without shoes are using hoof boots for riding on stony ground; there are several different designs so you need to take the time to find which works best for you and your horse.

Not using bits

Many riders nowadays are 'ditching the bit'. There's harrowing stuff on the internet about the cruelty of bits, which, if you believed it unquestioningly, would have you digging a pit to bury your bits in right away. However, as with so much in life, this is not a simple issue. Bitless is not necessarily kind, and its opposite (would that be bitful?) is not necessarily cruel.

One of the cruellest devices I've ever seen was a bitless bridle used on Peruvian Paso horses at a ranch in California in the 1980s. It was basically a bootlace pulled tightly round the horse's nose, like a sort of grotesque tourniquet, with reins attached all ready to pull the head up in good style. The animals I saw subjected to this barbarity were in a state of what looked to me like terror, but which the proud owner assured me was a desirable quality called 'brio'. Just the memory of it still makes me feel sick.

Many bitless bridles have to be tightly fitted around the horse's head in order to stop them slipping about. This must be uncomfortable for the horse; it also prevents him from moving his jaw, which therefore prevents the all-important relaxation of the jaw. There are also bitless bridles that apply leverage to squeeze the lower face and jaw; these are severe pieces of equipment as harsh as any bit.

An improperly used bit, or one that is of poor design, or doesn't fit or is wrongly adjusted, especially combined with a noseband to clamp the mouth shut, causes great suffering to a horse. You have to be careful with snaffles. The joint of a jointed snaffle, if pressure is put on the bit, will bump against the roof of mouth – agonising for the horse whose mouth is strapped shut by a noseband. The central link of a French snaffle, if it's a flat plate, can dig into the tongue, which is again agonising if the mouth is strapped shut. But an appropriate bit, such as a French snaffle with a small lozenge in the middle, correctly fitted and properly used is not a problem. In fact horses will actually seek out such a bit because it helps with the relaxation of the jaw and poll that horses find so delightful.

You can judge for yourself how willing your horse is to welcome the bit. (And be careful when taking the bridle off: don't just pull the headpiece over his ears and drop the bit onto his lower teeth – that would be enough to put anyone off!)

My mare Brigit, when offered a choice between her light Neue Schule snaffle and a halter, invariably chooses the snaffle. She loves to take it and mouth it gently and dreamily, her eyes going soft and her face smoothing into an expression of delight as she relaxes her jaw and flexes her poll. This is the key to correct use of a bit: it isn't an instrument of force, or even a braking system, but an aid to help you and your horse with relaxation, communication and connection.

There are some wonderful riders around nowadays, many of them findable via the internet, who are riding horses without bits (and even without bridles), and doing marvellous things, including inspiring their horses to offer collection at the highest levels such as piaffe and levade. They are demonstrating that a bit is not essential if – and this is a big 'if' – you're riding at that level. If you're not there yet, don't feel pressured into ditching the bit – both you and your horse might still find it helpful.

Spurs, whips and tie-downs

I would like to add nosebands to this list of equipment that requires careful, honest scrutiny. I'm particularly concerned about the widespread use of flash straps attached to cavesson nosebands to clamp the horse's jaw shut. They are not only cruel, preventing the horse from trying to alleviate the pain in his mouth from the bit; they are counter-productive as they prevent him from doing the very thing you want – relaxing his jaw. Even a plain cavesson, if adjusted tightly, will limit the movement of the horse's jaw and inhibit relaxation.

As to spurs, although they are horrific when misused, there are occasions when they can be helpful. The careful application of a small, blunt spur in gentle pressure-release can help an unschooled horse to understand the rider's leg aids. And, when riding at a high level, the tiny, tiny, moth-soft touch of a spur can give greater precision, rather like the difference between touching you with a fingertip or with the palm of the hand.

Whips: I don't like the word. It gives completely the wrong idea: whips are for hitting and hurting and punishing. But sticks are different: you can do all sorts of things with a stick, including leaning on it as a support. A stick is a convenient extension of your arm, and it can help you to communicate. If the horse is afraid of it, then you can't use the stick to communicate anything other than threats, thus rendering it useless as an aid. But to rule out any kind of stick is to overlook how helpful it can be if used properly.

Tie-downs can include martingales and auxiliary reins such as draw reins. I dislike draw reins and other gadgets used to force the horse into a particular position. Stretching exercises can be as useful for horses as yoga exercises are for humans, but we don't tie down human yoga students, and neither should we tie down horses. These bondage methods seem to me to be not only cruel but perilously close to sicky dominance nastiness, with a small human dominating a large animal – man's dominion over nature. In competitive dressage we commonly find the additional elements of a small female human dominating a large male horse, with marks given for the 'submission' of the horse; with the whips, spurs and bondage equipment already present, all we need to complete the scene are stiletto heels and scanty panties.

I must admit to being a bit sniffy about martingales. However, having not used one for about twenty years, I dug out a running martingale recently to put on a client's horse for the client's safety. Anna wanted to hack out on her mare, who had a habit of sticking her head in the air when over-excited. I didn't think the mare was ready to ride out, but Anna was determined to ride her horse and this was not the time to be fundamentalist about it – my priority was to keep Anna safe. A running martingale prevents a horse getting its head dangerously high or even smashing the rider in the face with the top of its head; however it interferes with your direct contact with the horse's mouth and also redirects the pressure of the bit downwards, which can be uncomfortable for the horse.

No tack at all

Riding a lovely cushiony horse bareback is one of life's delights. You feel so much closer without a saddle between you. Some people are taking this further and riding with no tack at all – no bridle, no halter, not even a neckstrap. I love the idea, and am experimenting with my mare Brigit, who is very steady and reliable. (I confess I haven't dared to try it with the Ginger Fizz; he's still too prone to firing up, and he seems to believe – erroneously – that the rider is super-glued to his back so that he can jump about with carefree abandon.) I have mixed feelings about the videos on the internet showing people careering about on 'naked' horses. On the one hand I find them wonderful, inspiring and utterly beautiful; on the other hand I think they should come with a health and safety warning – 'Don't try this at home, folks!' These riders are clearly highly skilled in their ability to stay on and also in their ability to understand and communicate with their horses. They make it look very much easer than it is – or at any rate very much easier than it would be for anyone less skilled.

Natural horsemanship training systems

Training systems continue to proliferate in the field of natural horsemanship. Some of them are very helpful; some less so. Sadly, some seem to have come up with more sophisticated methods of bullying horses. As with everything in life, you need to use your own wise discernment, welcome what you find useful, and leave the rest.

Often the system itself is not what's so important: a good horseperson is good whether or not she follows a system; similarly a poor one is poor regardless of how many levels of training she has notched up. Experience is essential, and attitude is more important than anything else. Love, kindness, empathy, steadfastness, patience and good humour... these are the qualities of a human a horse is happy to hang out with.

There's a wide and wonderful world of horsemanship out there and, wherever your explorations lead you, I wish you well on the journey. May you and your marvellous, magnificent horse enjoy every step of the way!

WHAT'S NEXT?

If you have enjoyed this book, and are wondering where to go from here, I recommend that you visit the website:

www.theconfidentridercoach.com

Here you'll find much, much more. For a start, it's not just for riders; it's for anyone who is interested in horses. There's a blog and lots of articles, some of them expanding on topics mentioned in the book and some on entirely new topics. There are photos illustrating points in the book, such as in-hand exercises. There's a membership scheme offering courses you can take, via the website, on subjects such as lungeing, long-reining and in-hand practice, plus a forum where you can meet up with other like-minded people.

There will soon be information about the next book, which is about going further with your connection with your horse. If you'd like to discuss anything in Heart to Heart with Your Horse, you're very welcome to contact me via the website. And of course you can also contact me for email or telephone mentoring, or to discuss the possibility of workshops, clinics or one-to-one coaching.

FURTHER READING

BOOKS

Magali Delgado and Frederic Pignon	Gallop to Freedom
Klaus Ferdinand Hempfling	Dancing with Horses
Gerd Heuschmann	Tug of War: Classical versus 'Modern' Dressage
Oliver Hilberger	Schooling Exercises In-hand
Linda Kohanov	Riding Between the Worlds
Linda Kohanov	Tao of Equus
Susan McBane	6 Steps to a Schooled Horse
Susan McBane	100 Ways to Improve your Horse's Schooling
Heather Moffett	Enlightened Equitation
Omar Rabia	Cobs Can!
Imke Spilker	Empowered Horses
Perry Wood	Dressage the Light Way
Perry Wood	Real Riding

WEBSITES

In addition to the websites of these authors, you might enjoy:

www.horseconscious.com

This has all sorts of marvellous things on it, including introductions to several outstanding and inspiring trainers.

www.theclickercenter.com

This is Alexandra Kurland's site, which has lots of fascinating and helpful information about clicker training with horses.

Printed in Great Britain
by Amazon.co.uk, Ltd.,
Marston Gate.